Powerful Wisdom

Kurt Arrow

RICARSON–HEWETT PRESS
NEW YORK

ISBN: 978-0615837550

First published in the United States of America by Ricarson-Hewett Press.

In loving memory of Theresa Kocsis,
also known as
Tessie, Mom, Grandma, Great Grandma and GG.
She was an inspiration to all!

CONTENTS

INTRODUCTION

re you one of the many people who are searching and searching for true, lasting happiness? Searching for answers. Trying to figure out why some people are so happy, without any effort. Are you always trying to understand your life and purpose?

Are you one of those people who keep on trying new things to find happiness such as positive thinking, raising self-esteem, relaxing activities, exercise, motivational reading, pursuing goals, spirituality, meaningful activities, play in addition to work, choosing to be happy, cultivating gratitude, fostering forgiveness and everything else the experts suggest? But you are still searching?!

You want to change your life, but haven't been able to come up with the answer that will set you free. Each new thing you try, you cling to like a life raft and hope and pray you've finally found the answer. And you want it to be simple and you want it immediately, right?

Do you often think that if you just achieve something like a new job, new attitude, new relationship, more free time, or something else, will be the answer. Sometimes the new achievements work out and you're happy for a while, but it never lasts, does it?

Have you ever wondered, that maybe you just won't ever find happiness, that you are born to suffer, that you have bad luck, that you are being punished by God for doing something bad, or anything like this?

And on and on and on you go, searching, but never giving up. You always have that little glimmer of hope. And that is why you are reading this now. Well, now it's time to STOP!

It's ironic that you have had the answer in the palm of your hand the whole time. Look at the palm of your hand. Do you see? When you look at the palm of your hand, you are right here in the present moment. All of your searching for answers was looking toward the future. All negative thoughts or the "baggage" that you carry, are stemming from your past.

But when your mind is focused on your palm, right here and now, you are happy and stress-free. Go ahead, look again and savor the moment. As soon as you start thinking of your problems (past memory) or dreaming of finding happiness (future), unhappiness returns, right? Don't worry, this is not about suppressing those thoughts.

Let's put it to the test right now. Stop reading for a minute and look around or take a short walk, focusing on everything you hear, see and smell and be aware of how stress-free and happy you feel right here, in the moment.

Congratulations! Your search is over! You found the key to happiness. Stress-free, unconditional happiness. I bet you are thinking that it couldn't possibly be that easy. Well, I didn't believe it either, at first. Your rational mind is telling you that it just can't be. And you are probably getting thoughts like, "Nothing is that easy," or "If it was that easy, everyone would be happy and stress-free," or, "I wish it was that easy."

Good news. It is, in fact, the answer you've been looking for. It is the key to happiness. Just by living in the current moment, you are happy and content. It doesn't matter what you have, where you are or what you are doing. It's with you all the time. You are inherently happy and stress-free. Just look at young children playing. They are stress-free and happy, and completely absorbed in the moment.

This doesn't mean that you never have thoughts of the past or future. It means that there are habitual thought patterns that pull you toward the past or future that are making you unhappy and causing you to search for answers, which is the very reason you haven't been able to find it.

Now, think about your happiest memories, or each time that you do one of your favorite activities, and how happy you are. While it's true that they are happy times and doing something you enjoy, the underlying reason is because you are living in the moment.

You already know that when you take your mind off your problems, you escape for a short time. Your mind doesn't know that it can be this way all of the time, like it did for the first few years of your life. As you grew older, your mind was fooled into believing that there is more stress as you get older, or more problems, or more difficult situations. Perhaps, you were told that by an adult, or two or three. It was fooled and that is why there is such confusion and searching for a better way.

The better way must be a way that your mind feels safe with. It must be convinced of that. It must be convinced that it is the answer. It is full of a lifetime of doubts, stemming from past memory or future, negative predictions.

INTRODUCTION

I'm referring to your mind as "it" because it seems to have a mind of its own. It's not what you want, otherwise you wouldn't be looking for an escape. So your task at hand is to change your mind. It is following a certain pattern of behavior and it can be changed by understanding the pattern and creating a new mind that will quickly and easily stop its self-destructive tendencies, permanently.

That is what this book is about. Essentially, you are battling your own mind to find answers that it just doesn't know exists (anymore), and you must now, get it to open up to see the truth and why it was fooled and why it changed from its inherent state of stress-free happiness.

Undoubtedly, you've heard of the phrase to "keep an open mind," and that is what you need to do right now. By keeping an open mind, you will allow it to absorb this new information that will transform it, resulting in true, unconditional happiness that lasts forever. It can be done and I'm confident that you will do it. You have too much at stake. You want to be happy from this day forward, right?

Trust me. You will do it just like I did it. I suffered for more than forty years before I was blessed with this simple answer I had been looking for, just like you. I battled depression and anguish of the worst possible kind, for so so long, only to find out that it

INTRODUCTION

never had to be that way.

Nobody should have to be unhappy. I have started a quest to help others put an end to there own suffering and live a happy life, starting this very moment. Right here, right now.

Life today demands that things be done lighting fast, doing it easily, and having it satisfying. That is my aim, to get you to find your true, inner self, quickly, easily and happily.

Our minds are very receptive to learning and exploring our world. But they are also very stubborn and set in their ways. They filter everything new to be sure it conforms to its pattern and is safe, so that it won't be subject to stress, anger or sadness. So it is a bit of a challenge to alter the pattern and remove the filter, until it is convinced it is safe to do so.

With that in mind, let's start right away, removing, or at the very least, easing some of your doubts, by telling you that this is not about brain washing. It is not about keeping a positive attitude, although it doesn't hurt to have one. It is not about hypnosis or memorization. It is not about will power or positive affirmations. It is not about learning my system or methods. It's about discovering your own.

INTRODUCTION

It is nothing that you are already familiar with. This is the tricky part because you have a natural tendency (pattern) to connect new information to something you already know. Something that you already know is safe. Something you already know that has already gone through your filter and is something you believe and trust.

If you are willing to allow me to be your guide, learn to trust me and keep an open mind, your mind will open to a whole new world that's still safe and secure. And very, very happy.

I can jump up and down and scream to you that it is wonderful, it works, it's safe, but it will always be filtered to protect yourself. That is perfectly fine and I have no intentions of trying to stop that. If you were trying sky diving for the first time, no matter how much I told you how great it is and not to be fearful, you wouldn't just accept that and jump without a moment of fear or hesitation.

Why should you trust me and what qualifies me to be your guide and teacher? Absolutely nothing! I have to earn your trust. I don't want you to believe anything just because I tell you. I have to teach you well, and let you draw your own conclusions.

I have already walked in your shoes of unhappiness and searching for a better way of life, a happy life. I have unwavering conviction that it works, it is safe and it is the answer, or the key, to unconditional happiness. And stress-free as well!

When my mind opened and it became crystal clear that it was causing its own stress and unhappiness, it left me in a state of mind that I never would have believed was possible. And one that I could never even convince my closest family and friends was possible, after I had achieved it. It is just too difficult for our confused and complicated minds to fathom. It is something that one must experience for oneself.

What you can look forward to, is no stress at all. None. Zero. You will no longer be able to cling to fear, anger or sadness, or any related negative states of mind that all cause stress. They still come up from time to time, but they leave moments later. It is complete freedom. But if you want to feel sad, you can choose to, and for how long you want it to last. Your emotions won't control you.

You will be able to control your emotions. Can you even imagine a life without stress and pure happiness all the time? Can you imagine being happy without having to buy something or go somewhere or do something or stimulate one or more of your senses to feel that way?

INTRODUCTION

Pretend for a minute, that you have complete conviction that what I'm telling you is true. That the key to happiness is living in the current moment. Doesn't that sound awesome? Such a simple concept. You don't have to search anymore. You don't have to struggle to make yourself happy. Just stress-free and happy. Just imagine...

You wouldn't be dwelling on the past. You wouldn't be worrying or fearful of the future. You wouldn't have to carry a grudge or hate anyone. Everything would be fresh, exciting and new – a first time. You wouldn't be trying to change your appearance. You'd be content as you are, and you wouldn't care what others thought of you. Can you imagine...

You wouldn't have to keep improving, getting better, stronger, smarter, happier. You wouldn't worry that you're not living up to others expectations, or even your own expectations. You can't stress out over anything. You aren't going to feel badly if you make a mistake. You are free to be moody or upset or act stupid or be an imperfect person full of faults. Can you imagine...

If another driver cuts you off, you don't have anger or road rage. Or if someone puts you down or makes fun of you, you aren't instantly angry and defensive. You would be clear minded and able to make quick decisions or be creative, inventive, write a book, solve problems right away. Wouldn't it be great?

You wouldn't have the "blues" or a bad day. No more craving for more excitement or a better life. Imagine feeling peaceful, calm and centered. No more boredom. You wouldn't have to try to excite your senses and your life. Imagine being in control of your emotions. You can feel sad if you want to and not that you have to. You can have ten things go wrong one day, and still be positive and happy.

Can you imagine being able to stop any harmful or unwanted addictions that you have? You would rarely get sick. You wouldn't get tension headaches. No tense muscles from stress. Wouldn't it be nice if your happiness was infectious and you're an inspiration to others? Imagine being a better listener and having a better memory.

You could always be one hundred percent truthful and others would trust and confide in you. You couldn't have an inferiority complex. You couldn't have jealousy. You would be much more outgoing and confident. Imagine all of your senses being intensely alert, especially regarding pleasure. It would be natural and not forced. Wouldn't you like to be in control of your life rather than life controlling you?

INTRODUCTION

How would you like to be content with everything the way it is, yet free to make changes if you want to? You don't have to imagine any of this. You can have it all if you are living in the moment, just like you are right this very moment. If you are sure that you want true happiness, then read the rest of this book. If not, and you are content to keep searching and hoping, and content to just find a quick happiness fix, stop here.

I hope that you will choose stress-free unconditional happiness, and if so, your new happy life starts right here and now!

INTRODUCTION

DISCLAIMER: All of the information, advice and recommended exercises are solely the author's opinion and are not written or implied to be used as a substitution to medicine, therapy or treatment by a medical or mental health professional. If you are currently under the care of such professional, it is recommended that you consult with him or her before reading this book. You may get intense feelings of euphoria, power and elation.

Whew! Now that the heavy stuff is over, let's get started!

CHAPTER 1

UNDERSTANDING CONSTANT CRAVING AND DESIRE

We all want inner peace, calm, tranquility and happiness. And yet we keep our minds churning with chatter. What she said. What he did. How to solve that problem. Those bad memories. When the next vacation will be. What to buy. Those money problems. The translation for all of this chatter is stress and craving. Craving for good feelings or craving to escape bad feelings.

The stress builds and builds until we either explode or find some way to relax, and it starts all over again. We like to blame it all on other people, our job, our hectic schedule, problems, negative memories or fears of the future.

We start asking ourselves questions like "Why am I so uptight?" "What's wrong with me?" "Why can't anything work out for me?" "Why can't I catch a

1 UNDERSTANDING CONSTANT CRAVING AND DESIRE

break?" "Why do I have such bad luck?" And then, these types of thoughts are stressful because they are questions without answers, and that leaves us with a feeling of hopelessness. So we get tired. Very, very tired.

The reason for all of this stress is craving and desire. Craving and desire is stress. The desire is to gain a certain feeling or desire to end a certain feeling. Ultimately, what you are trying to gain is happiness, and to end stress and unhappiness. Whether you have desire to obtain merchandise, desire for a person, desire for something good to eat, desire to engage in a certain activity, desire to get away, desire to gain knowledge or desire to achieve a goal, it is all for the same reason – to gain happiness.

Craving and desire never ends, does it? Sometimes you have a lot of desire and sometimes you only have a little desire. Regardless of how much, it is always with you, following you around like a shadow. That unsatisfied feeling. That feeling that something is missing from your life. That feeling of wanting a better life. That feeling that you are going to find happiness, or die trying. Sound familiar?

The good news is, you can completely eradicate craving and desire. Not by keeping a good attitude. Not with positive thinking or achieving a certain state of mind, all of which are fabricated and subject to cessation.   That would be like tearing off the top of a weed and expecting it to be dead and gone. But it will continue growing until you pull up the roots.

You are going to see exactly where the craving and desire is born in your mind, and you are going to see how it is sustained and allowed to flourish. After that you are going to learn how to stop it, once it is born. And finally, you are going to discover that it is completely dead and gone, leaving in its wake, a clear, peaceful and content mind. A mind that doesn't have to gain or get rid of anything in order to be happy and content. Complete freedom!

You are going to achieve happiness without craving and desire. Right now, you are probably thinking that, sometimes, you like to have craving and desire for something. If so, are you liking the craving and desire itself, or do you like getting what ever it is that you crave and desire?

I still crave and desire things, but in an entirely different way. It's a way that won't let me down, feeling disappointed if I don't get it. It's a way that I don't rely on it to provide my happiness. The problem lies in the fact that it is never enough. Once you get what you wanted, you either want more of the same, or you are on to craving for something else.

1 UNDERSTANDING CONSTANT CRAVING AND DESIRE

When you don't get what you want, you become very sad and disappointed. More stress. Disappointment leads to unhappiness so you begin to crave something else that will make you happy again. Do you see how the cycle keeps itself going, over and over again?

This is not about learning to expand your knowledge. It's about learning how to remove knowledge that you are currently convinced, that it is the way it should be. You are convinced that there is no escape from stress. You're convinced that there is no escape from craving and desire. You're convinced that all human beings are like this.

The truth is, that all human beings aren't this way and there is, in fact, an escape from it. People have been doing it for thousands of years. Unfortunately, a large majority of the living population is still stuck in the cycle, stressed out, and unhappy. Some, more so than others. I was one of them. I escaped from it. You can too. If you want to, you can.

You would think that everyone would want to be stress-free and happy, wouldn't you? You would think that this would be taught in school, and since it's so easy to understand, it would become prevalent in the majority of the population, and eventually be a new human race of happy people.

1 UNDERSTANDING CONSTANT CRAVING AND DESIRE

So why isn't it? Because the craving and desire is so strong, people's minds are diluted. Every time a desire is satisfied, although momentary, it reinforces the belief that it is a great working system that brings happiness. They live in a fog, unable to see that they are causing their own stress and unhappiness. And search and search for answers – for the key to happiness.

Thanks to people like me, who want to share the wisdom, people like you get to join the happy ones, the small minority of the population. I hope that you will choose to pass it on. I really hate to see people suffering, when they don't have to!

So how does craving and desire relate to living in the current moment? All craving and desire, all stress and unhappiness, are outside of the current moment. You would not desire something you have right here and now. You would desire something in the future. Something that you don't have yet. Did the light bulb go on for you yet? Did you get that "ah ha" moment?

Once craving and desire is uprooted, all that remains is true happiness. Pure unconditional happiness. The pure mind that you were born with. Once you have it, you will no longer have stress. Stress will be uprooted as well. And once you have it, it

1 UNDERSTANDING CONSTANT CRAVING AND DESIRE

can never reverse itself. You will be eternally happy.

Are you ready to end that constant craving and live stress-free and unconditionally happy?

The source of my wisdom stems from my enlightenment and a deep and profound knowledge of the source of craving and desire. I studied, for about eighteen years, the teachings of The Buddha, represented by the religion, Buddhism. Whether you have read any of the countless books and websites or not, and whether you are a practicing Buddhist or not, your own enlightenment is feasible and probable. You do not have to change your religion if you are not a Buddhist. All you need to have is an open mind and a desire to end desire, as crazy as that sounds.

Following my enlightenment, I recognized the need to simplify the Buddha's teachings and present the concepts from an entirely different perspective, in an effort to speed up the process of helping others put an end to stress and suffering, through there own enlightenment, right here and now. I have the utmost honor, gratitude, respect and admiration for The Buddha and his teachings, which are responsible for my own awakening.

I have been ridiculed by Buddhists for having my

own opinion and beliefs. But if they only really understood the Buddha's teachings, they would know that his message was that people should not cling to views, precepts and practices, rules and observances, and that would include his own doctrine and discipline. Be an island unto yourself. People love to cram their opinions and beliefs down your throat, and my advice to you is never to allow it, and stay true to yourself. They are not concerned with your happiness, only in preserving their own.

With this book, I am giving you my own teaching, which is more suitable to the current ultra fast paced American lifestyle, in a format of self-improvement rather than a spiritual or religious discipline. There are no right or wrong ways. You have to do what works best for you. But I am also going to give you some correlating Buddhist reference material as well. For about forty years, I have studied various topics related to psychology and self-improvement so you will benefit from my extensive knowledge of what works and what doesn't.

The Four Nobel Truths: There is suffering, Suffering has a cause which is craving and desire, Craving and desire can be brought to an end, The way to end craving and desire is to follow the Eightfold Path.

1 UNDERSTANDING CONSTANT CRAVING AND DESIRE

-BUDDHIST SCRIPTURES

We are always getting ready to live but never living.
-Ralph Waldo Emerson

Life is available only in the present moment. The present moment is filled with joy and happiness. If you are attentive, you will see it.
— Thich Nhat Hahn

You must live in the present, launch yourself on every wave, find your eternity in each moment. Fools stand on their island of opportunities and look toward another land. There is no other land; there is no other life but this.
-Henry David Thoreau

Happiness, not in another place but this place. Not for another hour, but this hour.
-Walt Whitman

All the Buddhas of all the ages have been telling you a very simple fact: Be, don't try to become. Within these two words, be and becoming, your whole life is contained. Being

1 UNDERSTANDING CONSTANT CRAVING AND DESIRE

is enlightenment, becoming is ignorance.
—Osho

Life is what happens to you while you are busy making other plans.
-Emily Dickinson

Life is a preparation for the future; and the best preparation for the future is to live as if there were none
-Albert Einstein

I am taking you down the path to enlightenment, also known as awakening and nirvana. What is enlightenment? The Merriam-Webster dictionary definition is "A final blessed state marked by the absence of desire or suffering." My definition is, an awakening to the reality of what life is, without our minds manipulating what we experience through our senses, without limits. If you ask a thousand people, you will probably get a thousand different definitions.

You are the only one who can possibly know what is going on in your mind, and you are the only one who can judge whether or not you have reached the exalted state of awakening. Be careful about what you read on the subject. There are plenty of people writing about how to achieve it and what it really means to be enlightened, however they are not enlightened themselves. There are even people, predominantly psychologists, professors and scientists, who have outlined all the various stages of psychological and spiritual planes, that one can possibly attain.   No one could possibly know that. They are either basing it on their own opinions or the consensus of many people. They are limiting their own potential and the potential of those who believe them.

True enlightenment goes beyond knowledge and the written word, and therefor cannot be put into words. And even if it could be put into words, who is to say that it will be exactly the same for all people? There would never be any new discoveries, or any new inventions or any new technological advancements if people limited themselves to what is already known. To that end, be cautious about what the "experts" say.

You may be wondering how I can write about enlightenment if it can not be put into words. That is a very good question. I am not going into detail of what enlightenment is. I am telling you how I and others achieved a higher state of consciousness,

1 UNDERSTANDING CONSTANT CRAVING AND DESIRE

and helping you on your own path to your own enlightenment. You be the judge if it is effective and you be the judge if you think that I am sincere. And you define enlightenment when you get there. Also, since it is an entirely different level of consciousness, the only ones who would understand it (if I were to write about it on that level), would be other enlightened people. So I am writing in such a way that you can comprehend it, assuming you are not already there.

I struggled long and hard to find it, only to discover that I already had what I was seeking. You do as well. We all do. I want to give you a brief history of my struggle for two reasons. So that you can conclude that if I can do it, you can do it. And to spare you from a long time struggle, so that you can put an end to your own stress and unhappiness quickly.

I was extremely unhappy in my teen years and decided to end my life. I took a can of plastic wood, which has a warning label that it could be fatal, and hid it in the woods in a place that would be impossible for anyone to find, so I could use it at a later date, if I was serious about suicide. I dug a hole a few inches deep, dropped in the can and covered it up loosely with dirt and finally, covered it with leaves, so it looked exactly like the rest of the woods that was covered in fallen leaves. When I returned a few days later, when I just couldn't live another minute, I located the spot, pushed aside the leaves and dug up the loose dirt, exactly how I had left it, but the can was gone! A complete mystery! I assumed there was some intervention from a higher power. I cried my eyes out and decided to live.

After the botched suicide attempt, my quest to find happiness began. Deep down, I knew it was possible, but I just didn't know how. I tried everything the experts suggested. I studied psychology and read countless self-improvement books. They helped a little. More than anything, they kept me motivated to keep looking and remain hopeful. I somehow battled through deep depression (caused by a chemical imbalance), personality disorders and drug addiction.

Around age thirty, I was learning the martial art of Aikido and there was a book in my dojo titled, Zen and the martial arts. I just had to understand the connection between zen, a spiritual concept, and the physical combat skills of martial arts so I read the book. That is how I was introduced to Buddhism. Of course I had heard of Buddhism and thought it to be a religion based on praying to statues of a fat man sitting cross legged with his eyes closed.

1 UNDERSTANDING CONSTANT CRAVING AND DESIRE

I later learned that the religion has nothing to do with praying to statues and that fat man was not the Buddha himself, who started the religion, but one of his followers who became a Buddha, which means, "Enlightened one." The man referred to as The Buddha was a thin man, named Siddhartha Gautama. He began his life as a prince in India but gave up his pampered life of luxury, becoming a homeless wanderer in search of answers of why people lived with such stress and suffering. While in a state of deep concentrated meditation, he was enlightened and found the answers. He then spent the rest of his life teaching others, in hopes of helping the entire human race. Although it was a philosophy, his followers turned it into more of a religion, and Buddhism was born around 500 BC.

I studied it as a philosophy since I looked at religion as an excuse for people to be prejudice toward others. After practicing for a few months, I walked into my kitchen, early one morning and something strange came over me. I can best describe it as a mini enlightenment. It was like I was in a movie or dream, in slow motion. I suddenly felt like I had great wisdom and knew all. I started thinking about teaching others, but then realized there was already plenty of literature of the Buddha's teachings. I slowly turned my head viewing objects around the room and realized that I didn't have to name them, such as, "salt shaker," or "basket," like I normally would. So they weren't separated from the rest of the room and its contents. Everything was beautiful.

The entire episode was less than a minute, and as quickly as it started, it ended, and there I was, back to stupid old me in a stressed out world. I quickly made some notes, on several scraps of paper and saved them,of what I experienced and what I had learned from it. I didn't know it at the time, but I had written the answers to my questions of how to be stress-free and happy.

It really encouraged me to continue studying Buddhism because if that was a taste of what enlightenment was, I wanted it! Regardless, my life got harder and harder, enduring all kinds of pain and suffering. I was homeless for a while, I spent time in a psychiatric hospital, lost my business, filed bankruptcy, lost my home, car and all of my money. I know, first hand, what mental suffering is. It got so bad, I often contemplated suicide.

Another fifteen years went by. Although I was still studying Buddhism, I still wasn't fully comprehending it. The teachings were not specific enough for me, such as, do this first, then this, etc. They were more of a, do all these things in your life, kind of thing. Live a "holy" life was the message. I decided to immerse myself in it, every waking moment. I observed every thought, every feeling, every emotion and forced myself to just be an observer and not to act or react. After doing this for about three months, I was at work one morning, focusing on the task at hand while simultaneously being aware of my thoughts and my mind suddenly opened. Everything became crystal clear. Enlightenment. My first thought was, "Oh my God, everything the Buddha taught was true. My second thought was, "There must be a better way to teach it, so people can learn faster."

As I was thinking about it, I remembered my notes from fifteen years prior, and when I got home, took them out and read them. One sentence read, "The Bible, Mathew 7:7 says, 'seek, and you shall find' and I say, find and you shall no longer seek." There were several notes about meditation and Buddhism, but the all important one read, "The truth, the answers, the beginning and end of time, are right here, right now." That sentence says it all. Fifteen years to come full circle back to a simple fact that set my mind free from the bondage of stress and suffering.

In each and every moment, there is birth and there is death. The world begins and ends. We use our

1 UNDERSTANDING CONSTANT CRAVING AND DESIRE

memories to create a sense of time and space, but it is merely an illusion. Like a mirage in the desert. We live in a dream and enlightenment is awakening from that dream.

If you truly want to awaken, and find true unconditional happiness, all that you need to do is commit yourself to making it happen, and continue reading. Don't be like a smoker who says he wants to quit but continues smoking "just a little" so he can pretend he is "cutting down to eventually quit." In reality, he is fooling himself and trying to fool others as well. Quitting is committing, period.

Imagine that you have a back pack on and it's so light, you can hardly tell it's on you. That represents a happy, stress-free life. Each stressful situation that you have is a ten pound weight that gets added to the back pack. Eventually, It gets so heavy, you are in severe pain and can't bear to carry it anymore. So you break down and cry, and you are forced to remove some of the weight. Preferably, you would want to remove all of the weight.

Now think about the stress you carry around with you all of the time, such as hatred, craving, worrying and trying to look good. Just those four would be forty pounds of weight in your back pack, all of the time. That would be difficult to carry around all of the time, right? In the same way, that is essentially, what you are doing when you are not living in the moment. You carry the weight of stress around with you and that is a heavy load.

CHAPTER 2

FINDING THE TRUE YOU

It is best to start with a clear mind without expectations. In other words, be open minded. When you open your mind, your mind will open. Begin with the knowledge that living in the current moment is, in fact, a really simple concept, and it is a really simple method to understand it and apply it in your own life. I am going to give you knowledge which you will use to attain wisdom. It is powerful wisdom that will free your mind of all stress and worry, leaving you incredibly happy.

I am going to be presenting to you, things that you are more than likely familiar with, but I will refer to them using a different name or description. The reason for that is to help you learn quicker, by lessening the chance of having preconceived notions, speculation or analysis. Normally, your method of learning is to continually add knowledge to your existing base. The problem with that here, is that your existing base is the main reason for your stress and unhappiness.

Up until now, your mind has been trained that when you learn something, you are gaining something, which is knowledge. Be patient with yourself as you learn an entirely new way to gain knowledge, which is by getting rid of something, like negative thoughts and habitual destructive thought patterns.

First, you will be gently introduced to making changes by simply observing your mind's behavior. That, in itself, teaches the mind what needs to be done to change its habits. Look at the rapid advancement of technology. Each new invention becomes a stepping stone to further advancement. The technology itself, makes the advancement possible. In the same way, your mind's advancement will point the way to further advancement. You will become increasingly aware of how you complicate everything. Not that you do it on purpose, it is simply the way you have been taught.

Later on, after you gain a deep and profound understanding how your mind behaves, you will recognize what causes stress and unhappiness, so that you can prevent it from effecting you. Most modern word processing programs on computers and phones automatically correct misspelled words, or at the very least, will highlight the word so you can manually correct it. That is exactly what your mind does. It automatically corrects your thinking if it does not conform to what it has been programmed with. That is why I say to keep an open mind, so that you can make a conscious effort not to let it revert back to its old habits.

If you are like most people, you have grown accustomed to doing activities or buying things that help to generate happy thoughts and feelings. But that is conditional happiness. It can only exist when certain conditions exist. Like everything else, conditional happiness is subject to fading away. You try to hold on to the feeling, which in itself is stressful, and that usually ends in major disappointment. That disappointment becomes your fuel to seek happiness again. And the cycle continues over and over.

Can you even count how many times you have sought happiness in the last week alone? You are going to learn to break the cycle and discover unconditional happiness, which is with you all of the time. It is with you right now, but you don't yet realize that. While you are reading this, try to subconsciously be aware how stress-free you are feeling.

I live every moment of every day in a blissful state of stress-free happiness that could never be adequately described, and soon, you will be too! I have written this book solely for the benefit of others and I am totally committed to helping you find true unconditional happiness, using ancient wisdom dating back thousands of years, applied to modern day lifestyle.

Happiness is right here, right now. You are inherently unconditionally happy and stress-free. You do not have to achieve it. It is with you all of the time. It is the true you. With a cluttered mind, it is impossible to see it. When your mind is uncluttered, the truth will be revealed to you. The key to happiness will be found. Like the old saying, you can't see the forest through the trees.

Doesn't it seem like you are just beyond the reach of true happiness? Always looking for answers. Always seeking out new ways to find and be happy Always trying to hold onto any happiness that you do find. Then, when you think you've found the answer, and you're happy for a while, it fades away. Or another bad thing enters your life and all the happiness is squashed. Or you might think that by continually adding new techniques, they will add up to the answer you have been looking for. Soon, you will understand why you don't have to look for happiness or try to hold onto happiness, because it is already deep within you.

Are you complacent just to be unhappy because you think it is part of life? Do you think it is because of your circumstances and the stress you under that it justifies your unhappiness? Do you find yourself bitching about everything, but then hate the fact that you are contributing to your unhappiness by doing so?

If you are driving somewhere new and you get lost, should you just keep trying to find your way? Or should you ask someone for directions? Or should you look at a map? If you answered that you should keep trying to find your way, that is not correct. If you answered that you should ask for directions, that is not correct. If you answered that you should look at a map, that is not correct. If you answered that you should do any or all of those options, depending on the circumstances, you are well on your way to finding the key to happiness, because you are open minded to all possibilities. This was a little test for you to determine if you are open minded or you have tunnel vision (I am not referring to the medical term for retinitis pigmentosa.) When I was about twenty-two years old, I was fortunate to have someone give me some constructive criticism. I was told that I only see things in black and white, and that I do not even open the possibility for the gray.

2 FINDING THE TRUE YOU

What is happiness? Happiness is being stress-free. What is unhappiness? Unhappiness is stress. Happiness and stress are complete opposites. And just as if they were on a see-saw, they always maintain their position, completely opposite of each other. When one goes up, the other goes down. When one goes down, the other goes up.

The more stress that you have, the more unhappy you are. And when you are extremely happy, you will not have stress. The True you, in a state of stress-free happiness, is to be found in the current moment, in the here and now. It is your see-saw raised all the way up. Stress on the opposite end is all the way down.

You probably have been taught, just like I was, that life is full of ups and downs and you just have to take the good with the bad. That you should, "roll with the punches," "stay positive," "take it with a grain of salt," "sometimes you will be happy and sometimes you won't." Does this sound familiar? While it is true that there are ups and downs as far as good and bad things happening, or at least, what you are currently perceiving as good and bad, it is not true that you have to just accept when it is dragging you down. There will be a lot more on this later, but for now, believe me when I tell you that we were taught the wrong thing. You can't control the bad things from happening, but you <u>can</u> control your reaction.

Whenever your see-saw goes down, that is when you are removed from living in the current moment. Luckily, your see-saw automatically goes back up, at one point or another. So you are always returned to the current moment of stress-free happiness. Think about the times when a serious problem or illness has been resolved. Or after you've had a really bad melt down and cry your eyes out. You return to the current moment and feel a great sense of relief, right? You always return to these three things which are synonymous: The true you, happy and stress-free, living in the here and now. Unfortunately, you don't stay there very long.

How about that awesome feeling on the first day of your vacation (after the stress of traveling to the destination) when you let go of all of your problems and stress melts away? The true you emerges. Even when doing drugs or drinking, you are brought into the current moment, happy and stress-free. That is why a lot of people become addicted.

Have you ever gotten advice to keep busy so that you don't think about your problems? If you took that advice, you became the true you, focusing on what you are doing in the here and now. Did you ever notice how happy you are when you are engaged in your favorite activities? Again, you are in the current moment, not thinking of the past or the future. That is an awesome feeling, right? The stress side of your see-saw is completely opposite and all the way down when you are in that happy state. That is what true happiness is. That is what you already have, and can feel that way all of the time, if you remain in the here and now.

It is not simply a matter of keeping your mind off of your problems and staying focused on the task at hand, and making a strong effort to do that. Like I said, that is automatic. You are already happy and stress-free in the current moment. What needs to be addressed is the reason why you are being pulled away from the current moment, causing your see-saw to change direction. You are not going to suppress all thoughts of the past or dreams of the future. You are going to learn how to let those thoughts come and go freely.

Living in the current moment, the here and now, is a very simple concept, but for most of us, it is hard to accept that it could be that easy to find true happiness. The reason it is difficult to accept, is that we are filtering in our memories of what we have learned (thoughts from the past) about stress and happiness, and until now, have never heard of something like this. We are also filtering in all of our failed attempts at happiness, which are also thoughts from the past. We also tend to filter in, negative predictions with thoughts like, "Nothing comes easily for me," or "I can't just stop all my problems," (thoughts of the future).

Don't worry about all those failed attempts at finding happiness. And don't think that all you have learned about happiness has been a waste of time. They are actually to your benefit. They are building blocks to understanding what needs to be changed. And they are positive influences on helping you cope with your problems as well as giving you the encouragement to keep looking for the key.

If you stay focused on what you are reading, right here in the current moment, then your life is about to change. Your mind has been conditioned to seek conditional happiness, through one or more of your senses. Like when you taste something you like, and you think it is bringing you happiness so you need more of it. Or when you listen to your favorite music. It instantly triggers a happy feeling and you want more and more and more. Conditional happiness fades away. The true you has unconditional happiness that never fades away. You will see what I mean shortly.

Not to confuse you, but ultimately, what you will achieve, is your see-saw stays right in the middle, completely level. You don't have the ups and downs. Even though you will still experience sad, angry and fearful times, you remain unshakable. Imagine that you are water in a drinking glass. Someone picks up the glass and tips it way over to one side, representing stress. You will see that you (the water) remain completely level like you started. If the glass is shaken causing a lot of turbulence, representing a huge amount of sadness, anger or fear all at once, you will see how quickly you go back to being completely level.

We are often tricked into believing that we have a problem right now, in the current moment. Think of one of your problems that you consider to be right here and now. Did your happiness decrease and your stress increase? Now ask yourself if this problem is something that occurred before this very moment (which would be from the past), or is it a problem that you worry about or fear the outcome or have a negative prediction of, (which would be in the future)? Or is it really right here in the current moment like you are trapped in a burning building? The only thing that is actually current is the continuous thoughts about it.

You might think it is a "current moment" problem,

but if you analyze it, it usually is not. Let's say that you are unhappy in a relationship. Aren't you unhappy about <u>past</u> experiences with that person, or is the unhappiness based on your negative prediction of the <u>future</u> that things are not going to improve between you? Or perhaps you can not make a decision about whether or not you want to end the relationship, due to fear (of the future) if you were to make the wrong decision or be left all alone.

One of the reasons that problems appear to be in the here and now is that we keep them floating around in our minds, thinking about them often, and it is the thought itself that is current, not the problem.

Here is another example. Your best friend thoughtlessly forgot your birthday and you feel sad. Your thoughts are memories of the past such as, "I did so much for his birthday and he doesn't even give me a call!" or "What kind of a friend (memory of past life experience) does that?" You may have thoughts of the future such as, "Some birthday this is going to be. I wonder if anyone will remember or care?" Do you see how that sad feeling only exists when thinking about the past or future? So it is bringing you stress and unhappiness by doing so.

I am not suggesting that you analyze everything. I

am only trying to help you see the truth of what I am telling you. If you live in the here and now, you will quickly gain the ability to spot stress and unhappiness even before it hits you. Remember that all stress and unhappiness is outside of the current moment.

At this point you may be wondering how to stop those spontaneous thoughts about the past or future. Or you may be questioning all of this because life does consist of past memories or future dreams, or you want to include that. I'm going to address your concerns. The problem is not the thoughts of the past or future. It is the clinging to thoughts of the past or future.

I am going to give you an easy three step system that keeps you focused in the here and now, as well as how to let go of unwanted thoughts, in just a bit. If you understand why you are unhappy and not realizing the true you, you will be able to make the changes that will reveal the truth. Keep in mind that there are times when you want to think about the past or future. It is the unwanted thoughts that are causing stress and unhappiness.

There are four human emotions which are happy, mad, sad and fearful. Since "happy" is constant (the true you living in the current moment) the other three are standing in your way of always being happy. Mad, sad and fearful are synonymous with stress. All stress is outside of the here and now. It is merely an illusion that they are in the here and now. This illusion has you in a state of constant confusion and bewilderment, which I call the false you. The confusion is what keeps you looking for answers and the key to happiness.

You may feel stress in the current moment, but it is the result of thinking of the past or future, which could be consciously or subconsciously. For example: You are angry about what Joe said behind your back. The anger would not exist anymore (in the current moment) if you stopped thinking about the past and what was already said.

Problems appear as if they are in the current moment, but they only exist when you are thinking about the past or future. Excuse me for being repetitive about this, but it is a point I really need to drive home. The only problems in the current moment are the ones you are solving right in that moment. The false you is what keeps you totally convinced that you need to keep them floating around in constant memory. The truth is, you will come up with solutions to your problems when your mind is not cluttered with all those thoughts floating around in there.

When you get those kinds of thoughts that take you away from the present moment, you simply let them go. When you let them go, stress drops and when stress is at its lowest, happiness maintains its position, completely opposite, at its peak.

At first, you may think that you will not have your pleasant memories from the past, or you will not be able to dream about the future or have future goals, if you let go of thoughts. Or you may think that you will become an empty shell without emotions if you don't have anger sadness and fear to some degree. That is the false you who thinks that. The truth is, your memory improves dramatically and your joy of living is multiplied a thousand times! You start enjoying even simple little things, without effort. Your mind clears so all of your pleasant memories and dreams of the future are vivid and spectacular.

You will decide when you want to think about a problem and solve it. The way it is now, you are not in control. It is like being in a rubber raft on a raging river and you are just holding on, trying not to capsize and drown. You are too scared to let go of the handles and grab the ores to help steer and balance the raft. Life is a raging river and it tosses you around. You can just let it have its way with you or you can take control of it.   Just like the handles in the raft that have to be let go of in order to grab the ores, you have to let go of trying to control your life in the same fashion you have been doing, in order to control your life and be eternally stress-free. And when you find that you have let go, your raft will feel like it is resting in a motionless uninhabited wilderness lake, calm and serene.

Habitual thought patterns, that make up the false you, run very deep and will cause you to keep questioning or doubting everything you are learning. That is a good thing. I am not trying to brainwash you or make you just accept everything that I'm teaching you. You need to be able to apply the wisdom in your own way.

Have you ever had a lot of stress, unhappiness or a problem? Have you ever had an issue that caused stress, unhappiness or a problem that could not be solved right away? And have you ever just tried to take your mind off of it, even just for a short time, by doing something enjoyable, even though it is not solved yet? Did you engage in a hobby, sex, eating, playing a game, watching TV, listening to music, traveling somewhere, or just keeping really busy with a variety of things (like the experts suggest)? Anything to take your mind off of the stress, right?

So at the time of your choosing, you switched from stress, unhappiness or thinking about a problem, to happy stress-free enjoyment. You are already doing some of the time, what you soon will be doing all of the time. You already know how to turn off stress (temporarily) like the flip of a light switch. Some people create their switch with drugs or alcohol. Some make the switch by burning off the stress with physical exercise.

What you are learning now, is how to stop stress from even developing. But if it does, you flip the switch which brings you back to the current moment which is stress-free happiness.

At this time I would like to empower you, for times when you really feel low and need a quick fix. I would like you to close your eyes and create a mental image of a black light switch on a white wall, with the switch in the "down" position. Now flip it to the "up" position and turn on the light. This is the current moment with stress-free happiness. How does it feel?

Now flip the switch back down to turn off the light. This darkness is where you have negative memories of the past or negative predictions of the future and it's where you will find anger, sadness and fear. The past and the future are in the dark and it is stressful trying to see them. How does it feel sitting in the dark? Think of something you hate and pause for a moment. Then flip the switch back up... lights on, current moment, back to happy. Now flip the switch down to darkness while thinking of something fearful. Then back up... lights on, fear gone, current moment, back to happy. Now flip the switch down to darkness while thinking of something sad. Then back up... lights on, current moment, back to happy.

Do this exercise a few times and really feel the emotions, and vividly see the switch as well as the light and darkness. This image of the switch will remain with you and you can use it as a safety net whenever you need to. This is just a technique you can use if you are totally down and out. Just until your wisdom and the true you has been revealed, at which time, you will no longer have to make an effort to change moods.

The true you, living in the current moment, is unconditionally happy and stress-free. Look at the following examples of living in the current moment, the past, and the future. See where you reside most of the time.

Living in the moment: Having a conversation, cooking, crafts, playing a game, having sex, writing/typing, visiting the doctor or dentist, going somewhere new, reading, fixing or assembling something, meeting new people, praying, meditating, practicing yoga, playing or watching sports, listening to music, playing an instrument, photography, painting, exercising.

Living in the past: Carrying a grudge, prejudice, hatred, thinking about a negative experience, comparing the past with the present, likes and dislikes, recalling who said what, arguments, gossiping, procrastinating, feeling bad about aging by thinking about how you used to be when you were younger.

Living in the future: Preconceived notions, worrying, setting goals or standards to live up to, trying to change appearance, predicting an outcome, daydreaming about the future, sexual fantasy, gambling, craving or hoping for something, telling lies, having expectations for yourself or others, wondering about your purpose or reason for existence, wondering about what will happen to you when you die.

Every time that you think about the past or future, you add a little stress to your life. And it adds up quickly! The more stress that you have, the more unhappiness you will have. Anger, sadness and fear are all emotions that are born from thoughts of the past or future. How much of your day do you spend doing that, thinking of the past or future?

There are times when you will want to think about the past or future and that is perfectly acceptable, provided that your intentions are positive and as long as you are not clinging to a specific memory or dream. Some examples are, planning a trip or event, recalling information (knowledge), fond memories or a positive outlook. At this point, you do not have to concern yourself with identifying what is acceptable and what is not. I am only laying the foundation of what you are going to be learning. Later on, you will get a better understanding of how your thoughts are pulling you away from living in the here and now, which is creating a lot of stress and unhappiness. I will also provide much more detail about clinging to thoughts versus letting go of thoughts.

Start to pay closer attention to your attention itself. You will see that, even when you are doing an unpleasant task, it can be stress-free, if your attention is focusing on the task at hand in the current moment.

Think about how much stress would be removed if you suddenly lost your memory. Everything would be new and you would see things as they are.

CHAPTER 3
OBSERVING THOUGHTS TO CHANGE YOUR LIFE

Just telling yourself to live in the here and now and let go of thoughts will not change the way your mind has been conditioned to behave. That would only be achieving knowledge. What you will need to achieve is wisdom, and the only way to achieve wisdom is through actual experience leading to discernment. Applying the knowledge will give you the skill to achieve wisdom.

There is a proven method or exercise that I call Thought Watching, which will reveal the true you. Simply put, you will just be observing your thoughts through heightened awareness. This process is designed to keep you focused on the present moment, right here and now, and make you aware of how controlling your thoughts have been. You will become acutely aware of how impermanent thoughts and feelings are and how you desperately try to hold onto or control them.

3 OBSERVING THOUGHTS TO CHANGE YOUR LIFE

Your thoughts which are generating feelings and emotions are constantly rising and falling away, as sure as your breath goes in and out. Some of your thoughts spontaneously arise and others are self-induced. All of our problems stem from clinging to thoughts. What I mean by clinging, is that you are trying to hold onto the feelings that are triggered or that you want to generate similar thoughts that provide the same reactions and feelings. We will get more into the intricate workings later on. Right now, you are simply going to observe your thoughts.

Thought Watching helps you to realize that you can take control of your thoughts to prevent self inflicted stress and suffering. You can not control spontaneous thoughts that just pop into your mind, but you <u>can</u> control your reaction. You can not control feelings and emotions that are instantly triggered, but you <u>can</u> control your reaction.

You may not be pleased to learn that you are the cause of your stress and negative states of mind, but you will get a great sense of empowerment when you realize how easy it is to stay happy and stress-free, and you maintain complete control. Most people think that it is difficult to control their minds and that is why I have simplified the method so it is hardly any effort to achieve complete control of your reaction to spontaneous thoughts.

When put into practice, you will have immediate results, that will give you the skill to let go of anger, sadness and fearfulness permanently. I want to clarify that you will still have these emotions but in an entirely different way. They will not stand in the way of your happiness. They will not cloud your thinking like they currently do. They will not rule your life, dictating when it is okay to be happy.

You are training your mind to stay focused in the current moment and to sense whenever you are straying away. You are learning that you do not always have to react to thoughts. You can simply observe them. Many thoughts suck you right in like a vacuum sucks in dirt. And you end up trying to continue a good feeling or repelling a bad feeling.

Thought Watching is three easy steps to help you identify the thoughts that are pulling you away from the current moment, the here and now:

Step one is OBSERVE. You observe your thoughts as they arise and how you react. Step two is ACKNOWLEDGE. You acknowledge what the thought is by naming it such as, "Angry feeling," or

"Thinking about the past." Step three is LET IT GO. You let it go by not trying to hold onto good feelings or repel bad feelings. It's a thought. It came. It's done and gone.

Remember that the true you, unconditionally happy is already there, so you will not have to make any effort to find it. You are going to observe all your thoughts and feelings by labeling them, exactly what they are, then you will let them go.

THOUGHT WATCHING

<u>STEP 1 – OBSERVE</u>

Live in the here and now. Watch everything you do, in the current moment. Observe how your thoughts of the past or of the future are what triggers mad, sad and fearful emotions. None of these are found in the present moment.

Observe every feeling that you get. Observe every thought that you get. Observe everything you taste, touch, smell, see or hear. Observe thoughts of the past, present or future. Good thoughts, bad thoughts, neutral thoughts, no thoughts. Just observe. Do not act or react to them. Just observe them. This step alone, is a gigantic stress reliever because it removes the need (or the habit) to react or solve a problem.

Observe how you have conditioned responses to almost every thought. A conditioned response is a pattern of behavior that is triggered by something you see, hear, touch, smell, taste or think, that instantly generates certain thoughts, feelings or emotions that are tied to it. It is your sense consciousness combined with your perception providing a result. These conditioned responses have become a part of your object of thought and cause restrictive thinking, often referred to as "tunnel vision."

When you read each of the following words and phrases, observe the conditioned response that you have. Observe the mental image and feelings that you get.

FUNERAL

SURPRISE PARTY

SCARY NOISES IN THE DARK

3 OBSERVING THOUGHTS TO CHANGE YOUR LIFE

FAILURE

YOU'RE A LOSER

CUTE LITTLE PUPPY

EXCITING AND NEW

THEY LOVE YOU

DEPRESSING NEWS

CAUGHT CHEATING

TRANQUILITY

With the first word, "funeral," breaking it down to its simplest form, is nothing more than a word. The word has a meaning which is the awful event of a person's burial. Now comes your conditioned response. In a split second you categorize it as good, bad or neutral. In the case of a funeral, it is bad. Then an emotion of happy, sad, mad or fearful is triggered. In this case, "sad." Then memories of the past or fears of the future might join in, and you have the cause of stress and unhappiness. So your conditioned response is more than just a word and its meaning.

3 OBSERVING THOUGHTS TO CHANGE YOUR LIFE

With the "Observe" step of Thought Watching, you are going to quickly learn how your conditioned responses are controlling and restricting your ability to see things as they are. Keep it simple and just observe. The learning aspect is automatic as a result of the action itself.

Observing your thoughts is just like watching a movie. Sometimes, you wish you could give someone in a movie, instructions or advice on what to do next, but you can't and you just watch to see what happens. You do not have control over what is going to happen in the movie and you do not try to hold onto feelings or repel them, since the movie will dictate that for you. You just watch it and allow it to be what ever it is going to be. That is exactly what you are going to do when you observe your thoughts.

<u>STEP 2 – ACKNOWLEDGE</u>

Just observing your thoughts is not very disciplined. So the second step goes hand in hand with the first, to help keep you focused and disciplined to carry out this exercise.

Acknowledge everything that you observe. This

will help you focus on living in the here and now. When you are not thinking of something that already happened, or something that has not happened yet, you will not be mad, sad or fearful. You will be right here in the present moment. This is where the truth, unconditional happiness and the true you can be found. Everything outside of the present moment is falsehood and that is where you will find sorrow, despair, anger, pain, suffering, fear, lies, deception, hatred and stress.

Now keep in mind that if you doubt anything that I'm saying here, it is not because I've written something unbelievable. It is because of your past memory and conditioned responses that your doubt is born from. There is no doubt or uncertainty in the present moment. Until your mind has been properly trained, which is what Thought Watching is for, it is possible that you won't completely understand or believe any of this.

Chances are that you think that negative emotions are happening in the present moment and that is true in a sense. But they are being triggered or born from a negative memory from the past or a negative prediction of the future. When you remove the past and future while in a negative state of mind, you will see it burn right out and die right then and there. Amazing and true! Look at the following examples for a clearer understanding:

Example 1: You are angry while having a heated argument with someone. Your thoughts are a memory from the past of what the person did or said that caused you to be angry in the first place. So now, you need to prove your point, to remove the blame for your anger and justify that the other person made you feel this way. You may also be predicting the future with thoughts like, "Now my good mood is destroyed so my whole day is ruined," or "I'll battle with you all day and night, if I have to. I'm right and you're wrong."

Example 2: You are at home and think you hear a burglar and you are scared to death. The fear is triggered by your knowledge (in the past) of what a burglar is and that it is something to fear. If there was a four year old child with you, would he or she have the same fear?

Example 3: Your best friend thoughtlessly forgot your birthday and you feel sad. Your thoughts are memories of the past such as, "I did so much for his birthday and he doesn't even give me a call!" or "What kind of a friend (memory of life experience) does that?" You may have thoughts of the future such as, "Some birthday this is going to be. I wonder if anyone is going to care."

Example 4: You go to a party, in a really good mood, until you spot that lady that you hate. Your mood instantly changes to a mixture of mad and sad. That is because of memories of the past, of why you have that hatred toward her. Or you may have thoughts of the future like, "Now I have to leave and my fun is spoiled." or "If she says one word to me, I'm going to lose it!"

Example 5: You have planned a trip to the amusement park for the past month. When you get there, clouds suddenly move in and it rains like hell. Your disappointment is overwhelming. It is because of thoughts from the past, when you were planning and imagining how nice it is going to be, and you pictured a bright sunny day. Or you might have a conditioned response (thought from past knowledge) that rain at the amusement park means misery. Or you may have thoughts of the future such as, "It is going to rain all day. It figures." or "So much for having a good time. Even if the rain stops, the rides are going to be soaked!"

Do you see how the emotions seem like they are caused by the current moment events, but they are triggered by thoughts of the past or future? When living in the here and now, you see it for what it really is, and without thoughts of the past or future, you remain in a happy state. It is not that you completely block them out. It is that you gain the ability to drop them once they come to mind.

The third step of Thought Watching is to "Let it go" which is after getting a thought and acknowledging what it is, you let it go and it's dead and gone. Before I go into more detail about the third step, I want to show you some examples of practicing Thought Watching.

In the following examples, the first step of observing thoughts is not shown, but you will see how they are acknowledged. The third step of letting go is also not shown but you can tell it was let go of by the next thoughts which are being acknowledged right away.

Example 1: The beginning of Tom's day

"Opening eyes. Struggling to wake up. Hearing radio. This body is sore. This back is killing me. Rubbing eyes. Feeling good, but a little tired. Remembering to observe, acknowledge, let it go. Getting a happy feeling. Sitting up at the edge of the bed. Turning off the radio. This body is sore. Cleaning corner of eyes with fingernail. Standing up. This back really is painful. Recalling what day it is. Thinking about confronting Stan about his comments. Getting an angry feeling. Started clinging to the bad feeling but remembered to let it go. Walking to the bathroom. Thinking about what I'm going to say without screaming or punching him. Anxious feeling. Closing bathroom door. Walking over to the toilet. Lifting the lid. Sitting on toilet seat. This back really hurts. Hearing a large truck go by. Feeling scum on teeth with tongue. Hearing noisy birds outside. Looking at radiator."

Do you see how everything that was observed is being acknowledged? Note that every time that you refer to your body or yourself, you never say "me," "mine," or "my." You are not taking ownership of anything that is experienced through any of your five senses including your thoughts. You may think that if you do this, you are going to become an empty shell without emotions. But the truth is, you will retain all the emotions, but they will not control you. Or you might think that by not reacting means that you do not care. All the clinging that you do, clouds your mind. You will actually be able to care much more once your mind is clear.

Example 2: Here is Maggie preparing to leave and then leaving her house to go pick up her kid from school.

"Grabbing keys and purse off of the table. Walking. Walking downstairs. Hearing phone ring. My land line phone. Turning around and walking back upstairs. Walking across the living room to the kitchen. Smelling something awful in the sink. Answering phone. [THOUGHT WATCHING IS TEMPORARILY SUSPENDED DURING PHONE CONVERSATION] Hanging up the phone. Hearing a siren off in the distance. Scratching itchy head being careful not to mess up hair. Picking up purse and keys. Walking, trying to leave the house again. Looking at watch. Worrying about the time now. Walking quickly down the stairs. Opening the front door and turning the lock. Checking watch again. Feeling rapid heart beat. Breathing heavily. Remembering what time I have to pick up Jen. Walking quickly to the car. Getting car key ready. Unlocking car and getting in. Smoothing pants as I'm sitting down. Noticing dirty carpet. Hearing more sirens. Starting car. Looking in mirrors. Putting shift into reverse. Backing out of driveway. Slowing down and quickly looking both directions before backing into road. Feeling badly that I should have completely stopped. Putting shift in drive. Stepping on gas pedal. Driving fast. Looking at my makeup in the rear view mirror. Sitting up straighter. Itch on leg. Turning on the radio. Feeling hungry. Changing radio station. Glancing at the time. Stepping on the brake, approaching stop sign. Coming to a rolling stop. Quickly looking both ways and gunning it. Thinking about what I'm going to make for dinner. Remembering to stay focused on the here and now. I can worry about dinner later. Stopping at light. Waiting for light to turn green. Looking at the time. Light changed to green. Seeing bird fly by. Feeling angry that someone is creeping along in front of me. Remembering to let it go. Looking at clock. Feeling stressed out. Pulling into school parking lot."

Example 3: Ellen, the night nurse, is making her rounds, going room to room that she is covering.

"Entering room 302. Going over to first bed. [THOUGHT WATCHING IS TEMPORARILY SUSPENDED DURING CONVERSATION] Dispensing hand sanitizer. Rubbing hands together to wash them. Leaving room. Scratching back of neck. Hearing moaning in room 306. That lady moans even if she's not in pain, and is becoming a big pain in my- Oops, hatred. Feeling happy that I caught myself. My mind is focused. Noticing pattern on the floor. Hearing my phone ring. Pulling phone out of my pocket to answer it. [THOUGHT WATCHING IS TEMPORARILY SUSPENDED DURING CONVERSATION] Putting phone back in pocket. Approaching nurses station. Checking the assignment list. Probably going to be talking to Tracy in a second. [THOUGHT WATCHING IS TEMPORARILY SUSPENDED DURING CONVERSATION] Well, she was sharing the latest gossip. Talk about not living in the current moment. Neutral feeling. Walking over to room 306 and not looking forward to it. Bad feeling. Turning on the light. [THOUGHT WATCHING IS TEMPORARILY SUSPENDED DURING CONVERSATION] She is so annoying. Bad feeling. Hatred rearing it's ugly head. Washing hands. Moving along to room 307. Hearing toilet flush. Scratching itch on back of neck. Fixing collar to see if that's what is causing the itch. Here comes miss personality. She'll probably have a big old attitude. [THOUGHT WATCHING IS TEMPORARILY SUSPENDED DURING CONVERSATION] I was right. Susan had a big old attitude. I don't know what I ever did to her to make her so mean to me. Letting it go. Observe, acknowledge, let it go. I want to live in the here and now. Knocking on door and going into room 307. Hearing toilet flush. Changing the name of the nurse on duty, on the erasable board. Waiting for the patient to come out of the bathroom. What an attitude Susan had. She really is a bitch. Bad feeling. Letting it go. Hearing bathroom door open. Seeing patient come out. [THOUGHT WATCHING IS TEMPORARILY SUSPENDED DURING CONVERSATION] Putting hands under foam dispenser. Washing hands. Leaving room. Closing the door. Hearing alarm for an emergency situation. [THOUGHT WATCHING IS TEMPOR-ARILY SUSPENDED TO FOCUS ON IMMEDI-ATE ACTION] Back to Thought Watching. A patient fell out of her bed and may have fractured her hip. Feeling tired and a little sad. Thinking about what I have to do when I get home. Thinking of the future. I don't need to think about that now. I want to live in the here and now."

Example 4: Jeff, a used car salesman, has just returned home after a long day at work. He is tired, hungry, and stressed out over financial troubles. What he says out loud are in quotes and his thoughts are not.

"Why the hell is the door locked?" Pulling keys out of pocket. Looking for the house key. Feeling agit-ated. Putting key in the hole and turning. Opening door. "Em? Emily? Anybody home?" Why would she be? Feeling angry. Or should I say, angry feeling? I guess it doesn't matter. Seeing mess on living room floor. Angry feeling. And hungry feeling. Opening closet. Grabbing hanger. Taking off my coat. Hanging coat in closet and shutting the door. "Look at that damn mess. Em? You here" Walking into kitchen. Seeing note from Emily on the counter. [THOUGHT WATCHING IS TEMPORARILY SUSPENDED WHILE READING THE NOTE] Out shopping... of course. Spending more money we don't have. Angry feeling. Hungry feeling. Opening the fridge. Spotting left over meat loaf. Great, another gourmet feast. She's probably buying another pair of shoes. It's okay for her, but she gets all over my case if I buy a damn toothpick. If I say anything, we'll end up fighting all night. I am starving. I mean, hungry feeling. Observing how angry I am, and letting it go. Or, trying to let it go. Observe, Acknowledge. Let it go. She's going to stroll in all happy. She didn't have to bust her ass all day, trying to make a buck. I couldn't sell my way out of a paper bag today. I can't believe that lady. Pretends she has the authority over her husband, to buy the damn car. Or was she just bullshitting me. Bullshitting the master bullshitter? I don't know. Thinking about the past. Observe, acknowledge and let it go. Focus, Jeff, focus. Right here and now. No stress right here, right now. Scooping up a piece of meatloaf and putting it on the plate.

3 OBSERVING THOUGHTS TO CHANGE YOUR LIFE

Smelling the garlic in it. Lifting up to nose to take another whiff. Let it go. I cling to nothing in this world. Nothing good, nothing bad. Opening door of microwave and putting it in. Closing the door. Hungry feeling. Setting the timer for three minutes and pressing the start button. I don't know how much time I wasted with that lady. Angry feeling. Thinking of the past. What's done is done. I should have qualified her right from the beginning. Angry feeling. Let it go. Live in the moment. I want to live in the here and now. Watching timer. Opening the door before it starts beeping. Touching meatloaf. It's barely warm. Closing the door. Setting it for two more minutes. I'm starving. I mean, hungry feeling.

With this Thought Watching exercise, you are learning to see each thought for what it is, before your mind manipulates it. Typically, you might have thoughts like, "That jerk really hurt my feelings. I would never treat him like that. Who does he think he is? That's okay, I'll get even." What you are going to do now, is observe and acknowledge "Thinking of jerk. Angry feeling." That is all. Nothing more. It was a thought that triggered several thoughts and a bad feeling. It is not yours and it won't upset you. You let it go.

3 OBSERVING THOUGHTS TO CHANGE YOUR LIFE

You will be rewarded all day long, for your efforts. Every time you remember to observe, acknowledge and let it go, you will get a happy feeling. You will be living in the here and now which is pure happiness. There is no time for worrying about your problems or the future, so your stress level will drop dramatically. You will feel lighter, like the weight of the world has been lifted off of your shoulders, and it will motivate you to continue living in the current moment.

If you are the type of person who worries a lot or clings to negative memories, you will continue to be that way for a while. You will be skeptical, uncertain and fearful of changing or revealing faults about yourself. You may even wonder if you should continue practicing. You will experience a lot of uncertainty. You will still be looking for that instant gratification and sense pleasures, so it is important to remember that this is exactly what is keeping you away from the present moment.

STEP 3- LET IT GO

This is the most important of the three steps.

3 OBSERVING THOUGHTS TO CHANGE YOUR LIFE

Thoughts are like bubbles in boiling water. The bubbles suddenly appear (your thoughts suddenly appear) then, almost immediately, they pop and disappear. Can you imagine the frustration you would have if you tried to hold onto those bubbles? That would be stressful, right? That is why thoughts are stressful when they are not let go of. When you are practicing letting go, you can picture your thought being inside a bubble as you let it go and watch it rise into the sky, until it is gone from sight.

Or you can do what I did in practice, which is to imagine thoughts like clouds in the sky. The clouds never stop. They drift on by, and so do thoughts, sitting on a cloud. Sometimes a lot of clouds fill the sky (lots of negative thoughts and emotions fill your mind) but then it rains as the clouds drift away and the sunshine returns, meaning the true you remains with its radiant joy.

For simplification, think of everything experienced through your five senses becoming a single thought. Sometimes the thoughts come at you in a rapid fire fashion, forming a group of thoughts. For purposes of letting go, think of groups as one thought. You observe it arise. You acknowledge what the thought is, or the feeling it triggers, and you let it go.

3 OBSERVING THOUGHTS TO CHANGE YOUR LIFE

If the thought is allowed to stay, new thoughts will stem from it, and you will open the opportunity to manipulate it, which you do not want to happen. If you were to hold onto a few bad thoughts in a row, you would probably consider it as being in a bad mood or having a bad day. The truth is, moods only exist when you do not let go. When you let all thoughts go, they weren't yours and your day isn't ruined. You remain happy, not to mention, stress-free.

With bad thoughts especially, you will be completely convinced that you need to keep thinking about them and not let them go. What you are doing subconsciously, is looking for relief from feeling so bad. And rather than being responsible for your own feelings, you blame others or say that you have bad luck. It's not your fault. Until now, you didn't have a choice. But now you have relief! Now you can let it go. It is a beautiful thing! Open the door to your jail cell and let yourself out.

Not only do you want to let go of bad thoughts, but you must try to resist the temptation to hold onto good thoughts, and let them go also. Let's say you get a thought, "Vacation is only three weeks away!" That thought triggers a happy feeling and you try to hold onto it. New thoughts stem from that such as

3 OBSERVING THOUGHTS TO CHANGE YOUR LIFE

"That's going to be so relaxing!" "Just the soft white sand beach and sunshine!" "No schedules." "No pressure." "That is going to be great!" "I can't wait." You are off in a daydream and it feels great.

Then all of a sudden, you CRASH! You are back in stress city. You end up disappointed and sad, that all those happy thoughts and feelings are over. It's an entirely different scenario if you had let it go. You would enjoy the thought that "Vacation is only three weeks away!" That is it. A happy feeling and you let it go. It doesn't lead to disappointment or sadness. You have been conditioned to seek pleasure of the senses. You never knew that you had happiness with you without trying. My words here, will not be enough to convince you of this. You will soon understand.

It is interesting to note that whatever thoughts you let go of, the complete opposite takes its place. If you let go of a sad thought, a happy thought takes its place. If you let go of anger, peacefulness takes its place. If you let go of jealousy, contentment takes its place. If you let go of fearfulness, bravery takes its place. There is one exception to this phenomena, and that is if you let go of a happy thought, nothing changes. You remain happy. That is the true you. Unconditionally happy.

3 OBSERVING THOUGHTS TO CHANGE YOUR LIFE

The more you let go of happy thoughts, it will become increasingly more apparent and your doubt will be replaced with conviction. You have been conditioned to cling to happy thoughts in order to keep the feeling going. That is conditional happiness. The happiness relies on the condition that you keep going with more happy thoughts. It is all you have ever known, so it is a tough habit to break. What you are doing now, is learning that you do not need to seek pleasure of the senses to make yourself happy. You already have unconditional happiness and the only way to realize that is to let go of all clinging. The more you do that, the more you will realize the truth and your mind will gravitate toward changing. That is one good aspect of its conditioned behavior, that it seeks pleasure. So this process of changing is easier than you may think.

How does that sound to you? Finding true happiness easily? Pretty good, right? Notice how good you feel right now. That is because you are living right here in the current moment. As you continue reading, try to notice how you are clinging to that happy feeling and hoping that what you read will keep that feeling going.

It is extremely important to let go of happy thoughts and feelings. Let go of all thoughts. You may think that letting go of all thoughts will change your personality or your likes and dislikes. You may think that letting go of your feelings and emotions will make you just a zombie who does not care about anything. It is simply not true. Your mind will be free and clear to have much more intense feelings toward yourself and others. You will not be tied down with your own stress and problems. Clinging to thoughts, whether good or bad, are always stressful because of the effort you are putting forth (subconsciously).

When you first learned to tie your shoes, you took it step by step and you practiced very slowly. The more times that you did it, the faster you got and the less concentration you needed. The steps eventually blended together and now, you do not even think about what you are doing. You tie your shoes on autopilot. You have a clear mind but you still know how to tie them. You can even think about something else while you are tying them. In the same way, when you learn to let go of thoughts, you will still retain your knowledge and memories, but in a clear stress-free way. It is absolutely awesome. You are going to love it!

To get what you want, which is stress-free happiness, you have to let go of what you have, which is clinging to what you have. Whenever you feel that you need reassurance, you can say to yourself, "To get what I want, I need to let go of what I have." For those times when you get completely over-whelmed with clinging, you can use the following phrases to keep in your bag of tricks, to tell yourself at the appropriate time for each.

I accept things as they are, not as I want them to be.

I accept people as they are, not as I want them to be.

This is a great opportunity to practice Thought Watching.

I don't cling to anything in the world. Nothing good, nothing bad.

I let feelings and emotions come and go, like clouds in the sky.

I accept chaos and confusion.

By being opened minded, my mind will open.

Observe, acknowledge, let it go. If you forget to practice it or have any difficulty with any of these three steps, then just loop right back to observe, acknowledge, let it go. It is to be expected. In the beginning, you will need to make a strong conscious effort. Trust me when I tell you that it gets easier as you go and it is well worth the effort! As you get closer to revealing the true you, it is possible that you will get intense feelings of euphoria, power and elation. Be sure to harness the feeling and observe, acknowledge, let it go.

I would like you to practice Thought Watching diligently for three entire days before going on to Chapter Four. Bookmark the page and leave the book where you can see it every day. Take note of how much you are craving to continue reading. This is an important aspect toward acquiring wisdom and not just knowledge. Observe the craving, acknowledge it, "craving" and let it go.

A monk lives contemplating the body in the body, ardent, clearly comprehending and mindful, having overcome, in this world, covetousness and grief; he lives contemplating feelings in feelings, ardent, clearly comprehending and mindful, having overcome, in this world, covetousness and grief; he lives contemplating consciousness in consciousness, ardent, clearly comprehending and mindful, having overcome, in this world, covetousness and grief; he lives contemplating mental objects in mental objects, ardent, clearly comprehending and mindful, having overcome, in this world, covetousness and grief.

Just as a skillful turner or turner's apprentice, making a long turn, knows, "I am making a long turn," or making a short turn, knows, "I am making a short turn," just so the monk, breathing in a long breath, knows, "I am breathing in a long breath"; breathing out a long breath, he knows, "I am breathing out a long breath"; breathing in a short breath, he knows, "I am breathing in a short breath"; breathing out a short breath, he knows, "I am breathing out a short breath." "Experiencing the whole (breath-) body, I shall breathe in," thus he trains himself. "Experiencing the whole (breath-) body, I shall breathe out," thus he trains himself. "Calming the activity of the (breath-) body, I shall breathe in," thus he trains himself. "Calming the activity of the (breath-) body, I shall breathe out," thus he trains himself.

Thus he lives contemplating the body in the body internally, or he lives contemplating the body in the body externally, or he lives contemplating the body in the body internally and externally. he lives contemplating origination factors in the body, or he lives contemplating dissolution factors in the body, or he lives contemplating origination-and-dissolution factors in the body. Or his mindfulness is established with the thought: "The body exists," to the extent necessary just for knowledge and mindfulness, and he lives detached, and clings to nothing in the world. Thus also, monks, a monk lives contemplating the body in the body.

And further, monks, a monk knows, when he is going, "I am going"; he knows, when he is standing, "I am standing"; he knows, when he is sitting, "I am sitting"; he knows, when he is lying down, "I am lying down"; or just as his body is disposed so he knows it. In going forward and back, applies clear comprehension; in looking straight on and looking away, he applies clear comprehension; in bending and in stretching, he applies clear comprehension; in wearing robes and carrying the bowl, he applies clear comprehension; in eating, drinking, chewing and savoring, he applies clear comprehension; in walking, in standing, in sitting, in falling asleep, in waking, in speaking and in keeping silence, he applies clear comprehension.

When experiencing a pleasant feeling knows, "I experience a pleasant feeling"; when experiencing a painful feeling, he knows, "I experience a painful feeling"; when experiencing a neither-pleasant-nor-painful feeling," he knows, "I experience a neither-pleasant-nor-painful feeling." When experiencing a pleasant worldly feeling, he knows, "I experience a pleasant worldly feeling"; when experiencing a pleasant spiritual feeling, he knows, "I experience a pleasant spiritual feeling"; when experiencing a painful worldly feeling, he knows, "I experience a painful worldly feeling"; when experiencing a painful spiritual feeling, he knows, "I experience a painful spiritual feeling"; when experiencing a neither-pleasant-nor-painful worldly feeling, he knows, "I experience a neither-pleasant-nor-painful worldly feeling"; when experiencing a neither-pleasant-nor-painful spiritual feeling, he knows, "I experience a neither-pleasant-nor-painful spiritual feeling."

Thus he lives contemplating feelings in feelings internally, or he lives contemplating feelings in feelings externally, or he lives contemplating feelings in feelings internally and externally. He lives contemplating origination factors in feelings, or he lives contemplating dissolution factors in feelings, or he lives contemplating origination-and-dissolution factors in feelings. Or his mindfulness is established with the thought, "Feeling exists," to the extent necessary just for knowledge and mindfulness, and he lives detached, and clings to nothing in the world. Thus, monks, a monk lives contemplating feelings in feelings.

A monk knows the consciousness with lust, as with lust; the consciousness without lust, as without lust; the consciousness with hate, as with hate; the consciousness without hate, as without hate; the consciousness with ignorance, as with ignorance; the consciousness without ignorance, as without ignorance; the shrunken state of consciousness, as the shrunken state; the distracted state of consciousness, as the distracted state; the developed state of consciousness as the developed state; the undeveloped state of consciousness as the undeveloped state; he state of consciousness with some other mental state superior to it, as the state with something mentally higher; the state of consciousness with no other mental state superior to it, as the state with nothing mentally higher; the concentrated state of consciousness, as the concentrated state; the non-concentrated state of consciousness, as the non-concentrated state; the freed state of consciousness, as the freed state; and the non-freed state of consciousness as the non-freed state.

Thus he lives contemplating consciousness in consciousness internally, or he lives contemplating consciousness in consciousness externally, or he lives contemplating consciousness in consciousness internally and externally.

He lives contemplating origination factors in consciousness, or he lives contemplating dissolution-factors in consciousness, or he lives contemplating origination-and-dissolution factors in consciousness. Or his mindfulness is established with the thought, "Consciousness exists," to the extent necessary just for knowledge and mindfulness, and he lives detached, and clings to nothing in the world.

Just as the royal frontier fortress has a gate-keeper — wise, experienced, intelligent — to

keep out those he doesn't know and to let in those he does, for the protection of those within and to ward off those without; in the same way a disciple of the noble ones is mindful, highly meticulous, remembering & able to call to mind even things that were done & said long ago. With mindfulness as his gatekeeper, the disciple of the noble ones abandons what is unskillful, develops what is skillful, abandons what is blameworthy, develops what is blameless, and looks after himself with purity.
-BUDDHIST SCRIPTURES

In the end, just three things matter: How well we have lived, how well we have loved, how well we have learned to let go
-Jack Kornfield

As long as we have practiced neither concentration nor mindfulness, the ego takes itself for granted and remains its usual normal size, as big as the people around one will allow.
-Ayya Khema

While washing the dishes one should only be

washing the dishes, which means one should be completely aware of the fact that one is washing the dishes. At first glance, that might seem a little silly. Why put so much stress on a simple thing? But that is precisely the point. The fact that I am standing there and washing these bowls is a wondrous reality. I am completely myself, following my breath,conscious of my presence, and conscious of my thoughts and actions. There is no way I can be tossed around mindlessly like a bottle slapped here and there on the waves.
-Thich Nhat Hanh

Mindfulness means paying attention in a particular way; on purpose, in the present moment,and non-judgmentally.
-Jon Kabat-Zinn

Mindfulness can be summed up in two words: pay attention. Once you notice what you are doing, you have the power to change it.
-Michelle Burford

Mindfulness is being aware of yourself, others,

and your surroundings in the moment. When consciously and kindly focusing awareness on life as it unfolds minute by precious minute, you are better able to savor each experience. Also, being closely attentive gives you the opportunity to change unwise or painful feelings and responses quickly. In fact, being truly present in a mindful way is an excellent stress reducer and, because of that, can be seen as consciousness conditioning, a strengthening workout for body, mind, heart, and spirit.
-Sue Patton Thoele

Without mindful awareness, the shadows of your past may haunt your present.
-Reuben Lowe

When we are mindful of everything we are experiencing in the present moment, we separate our awareness from our thoughts.
-Master Nomi

If my awareness of the past and future makes me less aware of the present, I must begin to wonder whether I am actually living in the real world.

-Alan Watts

CHAPTER 4

IDENTIFYING AND STRENGTHENING WEAKNESSES

You are gaining great insight into your thought patterns when you practice Thought Watching. Now I want to introduce you to another exercise, called Breath Watching, for an even deeper understanding of how your thoughts and feelings are constantly coming and going. When they are left alone, you are completely free of their control over you.

Breath Watching is an exercise that will improve your concentration and conviction that the true you can, and will, be revealed. It will help you to stay focused and to live in the here and now. It will also speed your progress in this whole process of identifying and eradicating the false you. In other words, it will identify what is causing your unhappiness. Best of all, it relaxes you and relieves stress. You are going to experience all of your emotions coming and going, and get a thorough understanding of just how impermanent thoughts are. This exercise also trains your mind to just observe thoughts and not react, which is key to gaining control.

Make yourself comfortable, sitting or laying down, in a quiet location. Choose a part of the day when you are most energetic and alert. You want to relax your body but remain mentally alert. Close your eyes and remain focused on the tip of your nose. Feel the air moving in and out of your nose as you breathe. The only thing in the world that exists is your breathe, right here in the current moment. Think, "Breathing in... breathing out. Breathing in... breathing out. Breathing in long... breathing out long. Breathing in... breathing out. Breathing in shaky... breathing out shaky. Breathing in... breathing out. Breathing in... breathing out. You'll notice how different each breath is and you should identify it.

When you observe a thought pop up, acknowledge it by saying, "Thinking," then let it go, and go right back to saying, "Breathing in... breathing out. When you first start doing this Breath Watching exercise, you will probably be flooded with thoughts. They will distract you, and pull you off in a daydream. This will happen often. Acknowledge by saying, "Thinking," let it go, then return to saying, "Breathing in... breathing out."

It is common for people to think that they just cannot do this exercise, and get very frustrated. Just observe that frustration and negativity, acknowledge it, and let it go. It is perfect just the way it is. It is a learning curve that gets easier and easier each session. If you get an itch or a pain, just observe how suddenly it pops into existence and will probably end within a few seconds. Try your hardest not to scratch an itch. Observe how lots of bodily feelings are coming and going all of the time.

As your concentration improves, you will get increasingly more focused on only the breath, and you will go through different states of consciousness, until you go beyond consciousness and all that you are experiencing is pure emptiness. Thoughts completely stop, breathing is almost non existent and you will have no bodily feelings as if you are floating in air.

You do not have to work at achieving higher levels of concentration and states of consciousness. It happens all by itself. If you start making a conscious effort to change your states of mind, then you will no longer be focused on the breath and the breath alone, and it will hinder your progress! Be patient. Once you know how relaxing and pleasurable it is, resist craving for it. But you should observe that craving, acknowledge it and let it go, the same as you do during your daily Thought Watching. Observe, acknowledge, let it go.

Try to do this Breath Watching exercise two to four times weekly. Each session should be at least an hour, with no restriction on how long. I like a two hour session. If you are unable to settle your thoughts, even a little, after forty-five minutes, do not try to force it. Just try another time. It is okay. This will happen occasionally.

If you are distracted because you are trying not to forget things that you have to do later, just make a note or a "to do" list before you begin your Breath Watching session. You can also write down things that you are worrying about to help clear your mind before you get started.

Most importantly, do not grade yourself by making statements like, "That was a terrible session," or "I'm not making any progress," or "I'm not good at this." Even what you consider negative experiences are great learning experiences and a prime opportunity to observe those negative feelings and emotions, acknowledge them and let them go.

4 IDENTIFYING AND STRENGTHENING WEAKNESSES

I trust that you are vigilant about practicing Thought Watching as much as you can, every day. When you "acknowledge" the thought, it helps to simply identify the thought without judgment, and do it in a way that ends it right then and there. Look at the following examples of the right and the wrong way to "acknowledge" thoughts and feelings. Observe how every statement that is the wrong way, which are shown in parenthesis, opens the door for additional thoughts. Those thoughts would probably be negative, giving you stress, pain and suffering. It also makes it much more difficult to "let it go."

THOUGHT (wrong way to acknowledge) Right way

NEW PHONE (I want a new phone) Desire

UNLUCKY (Why do I have such bad luck?) Negative thought

I AM SAD (I feel miserable today) Sad feeling

ANGRY (She really pissed me off) Angry feeling

LUCKY FOR HIM (He has such good luck) Jealousy

LOTS OF STRESS (I am so stressed out) Stressful feeling

SORE NECK (My neck is sore) Painful feeling

LONG LINE (Hope I don't have to wait) Negative thought

HUNGRY (I am starving) Hungry feeling

GOOD LOOKING GIRL (There's a hot babe) Sensual desire

TOO MUCH WORK (I have no free time) Negative thought

WHAT HE SAID (I can't believe he said that) Thinking of the past

Any negative thoughts, or thoughts in the categories of mad, sad or fearful, which are thoughts of the past or future, all are preventing you from realizing the true you. The Thought Watching process is going to evolve to a point where your mind quickly foresees your acknowledgment and detects the error of its way.

The right way to acknowledge thoughts is to simply

identify what the thought is without taking ownership of it as my thought or my feelings, thereby
remaining in a stress-free happy and content state –
the true you. It is far easier to let go of thoughts
that do not belong to you. They are just thoughts
and nothing more.

If "happy" is what you want, you need to let go of
"mad," "sad," and "fearful." Here is a closer look
to help you identify what falls into those three categories. So if any of these characteristics describe
you, then you are not living in the here and now.
Each of these are caused by thoughts of the past or
future.

MAD: Angry, bothered by making mistakes,
aggravated, judgmental, agitated, pessimistic,
annoyed, certain thoughts of the past, critical of others, egotistical, feelings of inferiority, complainer,
hatred/prejudice, certain thoughts of craving and
desire, feelings of stupidity, argumentative, harmful
addictions, vindictive, mean, lustful, opinionated,
spiteful, tattletale, cheater.

SAD: Disappointed, feelings of failure, making
mistakes, certain thoughts of craving and desire,
negative self worth, negative predictions, negative
news announcer, pessimistic, egotistical, feelings of

stupidity, harmful addictions, opinionated, certain thoughts of the past.

FEARFUL: Negative predictions, preconceived notions, certain thoughts of the future, certain thoughts of craving and desire, know-it-all, thoughtless, paranoid, judgmental, argumentative, absent minded, obsessive-compulsive, regretful, procrastination, stubbornness, selfish, opinionated, secretive.

The following are some of the common habitual patterns that inhibit the ability to stay stress-free and happy, as well as live in the current moment. Are you any of these?

WORRYING ALL THE TIME: Are you always worrying about problems or future situations? If so, you are fearful of events not working out perfectly, which ultimately means stress and unhappiness. You do not realize that you are causing stress and unhappiness in the current moment, because you are trying to prevent it in the future. Worrying also means that you are trying to control everything like you are directing a movie. Things are going to happen, good or bad, whether you worry about them or not.   You know that deep down, but worrying always seems to take a hold of you and you are helpless to stop it, once it begins, or prevent it in the first place. You are fooled into believing that worrying helps so that the problems don't take you by surprise.

When you live in the here and now, there is nothing to worry about. Your mind clears so that you can solve those problems that can be solved right away. If it is a problem that can not be solved right away, and you have done all that you can toward solving it, then leave it for the future. You can create a "Problems" pad and make a note of it, in order to take it out of your mind. You can even have a problem solving time, set aside each week, to take out your notes and see if you can work on any of the problems at that time. When practicing Thought Watching and you "observe" worrying beginning, then "acknowledge" it by saying, "worrying," and "let it go."

Your habit of worrying has a strong hold on you. You may be observing and acknowledging a lot of worrying all day long. It may seem a bit hopeless that you will never be able to stop it. Trust me, you will be able to stop it. Just keep acknowledging it, saying,"worrying," even if it is every two minutes. Every time that you do, and then let it go, you will feel great that you do, in fact, have control and you will feel great living in the here and now. Your mind gravitates toward feeling great so it will take care of it without a lot of effort, other than acknowledging and letting go.

SELF HATRED: If you hate yourself, you probably hate other people too. I am sure you have heard the phrase that you can not love someone else if you do not love yourself. People usually hate about others, the very same things they hate about themselves. When you hate yourself, you are angry. When you hate other people, you are angry. The angry emotion is outside of the here and now. You have either created an image of how you want to be, based on what you have seen or heard in the past, or what you want to become in the future.

You are probably comparing yourself to other people. And the people you compare with are the ones who you think are perfect. If you ask any of those "perfect" people if they like themselves, you will probably learn that most of them hate themselves also. Stay in the current moment and you are perfect just as you are. Every single person is full of imperfections, both physically and mentally. You look at that beautiful "perfect" woman and when she opens her mouth to speak, her teeth are crooked and yellow and she sounds like mini mouse.

4 IDENTIFYING AND STRENGTHENING WEAKNESSES

Your vision of what you want to be, may not be as awesome as you think. Let's say that you wanted to be good looking like a model and you had the ability to just snap your finger and change yourself. So now, you have the perfect look. Since life goes on, you will age and your perfect look will deteriorate. Then you have the challenge of maintaining your perfect complexion and your weight. And naturally, you need the perfect wardrobe to accentuate your perfect look. You also need to worry about your hair and your teeth. How you walk and how you talk. Do you see how much stress you will have, trying to maintain that perfection?

We all have good and bad qualities. When you just accept yourself the way you are, you remove the anger and you realize, it is better to be ugly and happy than beautiful and stressed out and miserable. Self hatred is just another form of craving and desire. You are craving to end the way you are now and desire to become something else. And that is exactly what keeps the wheel of unhappiness turning.

No matter what age you are, or what your circumstances might be, you are special, and you still have something unique to offer. Your life, because of who you are, has meaning.

4 IDENTIFYING AND STRENGTHENING WEAKNESSES

- Barbara de Angelis

What you think about yourself is much more important than what others think of you.
- Marcus Annaeus Seneca

Friendship with oneself is all-important, because without it one cannot be friends with anyone else.
- Eleanor Roosevelt

I didn't belong as a kid, and that always bothered me. If only I'd known that one day my differentness would be an asset, then my early life would have been much easier.
- Bette Midler

The greatest success is successful self-acceptance.
- Ben Sweet

AVOIDING THE HERE AND NOW: You are constantly busy. Busy on your cell phone or your computer. Or you are busy watching television. Or you are busy playing video games, or you are talking with others about the past or future. You may not even be aware that you are trying to avoid the here and now. The reason that you do not want to be in the present moment is based on fear. You are fearful of having to face your problems, or stress or unhappiness. By keeping your mind preoccupied, you get to pretend that you are stress-free and happy. But when you are forced to deal with an issue right away, it is like being stuck with a hot poker. You may even have a bit of a breakdown.

Unfortunately, this behavior reinforces your belief that the present moment must be avoided. The conditional happiness, that you currently have, just masks your problems, stress and unhappiness. The fear of living in the here and now is only because you are not living in the here and now. Remember that the emotion of fear is one of the three emotions that are all outside of the here and now. Mad, sad and fearful. Once you begin living in the current moment, you will discover that there is no fear to be found. There is no stress and unhappiness in the here and now. If you have been avoiding it, living in the moment will be an incredible surprise.

F E A R is False Evidence that Appears Real.

4 IDENTIFYING AND STRENGTHENING WEAKNESSES

-Anthony Robbins

BLAMING EVERYTHING OR OTHER PEOPLE FOR YOUR UNHAPPINESS: Take a moment to think about your current, major reason for your stress or unhappiness. If you suddenly lost your memory, would you still have the same amount of stress or unhappiness over it? Think about it.

Imagine that you lost your memory, but did not realize that you lost it. Would you still have the same amount of stress or unhappiness? What if you suddenly lost your ability to worry about or think about the future, also? So you have no memory of the past and you cannot think about what might happen in the future. You are in the current moment and that is all you know. Do you still have the same amount of stress or unhappiness?

Can you see how it is your own doing, bringing on the stress or unhappiness? It is the way you are reacting to the situation. Circumstances and people do not cause stress or unhappiness. If you are brave enough to admit it, if you are strong enough to take responsibility for it, you will find it easier to learn how to prevent it. You are responsible for how you feel, and you are the person who can change the way you feel about a particular situation.

A lot of what you experience is not as it appears. The more you live in the here and now, the clearer it becomes. Consider the following examples.

THERE IS NO SUCH THING AS A PROBLEM. It is the inability to see things clearly. It is merely a challenge. A problem is something that you just don't have an immediate solution for. Problems seem worse when you are worrying about them. Try to just accept the fact that it doesn't have an immediate solution.

THERE IS NO SUCH THING AS A STRESSFUL SITUATION. What is stressful is thinking about the past or the future. There is no stress in the here and now. You may have created a vision of the perfect scenario of how the situation should be, so you are comparing the past with the present.

THERE IS NO SUCH THING AS BAD LUCK. Thinking this way comes from basing an outcome on a predetermined standard, stemming from a thought from the past. Each event, each moment, is separate from all other events or moments. But if you group all the bad events together, then you have a bunch of bad events, not bad luck. With this line of reasoning, that a bunch of bad events are bad luck, then you also have good luck when you bunch good events together. What has happened in the past doesn't mean it will happen in the future.

THERE IS NO SUCH THING AS HATRED: This is people's way of medicating why they are feeling so bad. Clinging to thoughts from the past are the reason for the hatred itself. Because of the laws of karma (more on this later), every time that you have thoughts of hatred, you will feel bad, and that is your own fault, not the person that you hate.

THERE IS NO SUCH THING AS A BAD MOOD. This is multiple thoughts of the past or future causing anger, sadness or or fear that are considered bad. Clinging to thoughts and grouping them together gives the illusion of being in a certain mood, be it good or bad.

Be consciously aware of all of your faults and shortcomings. When you are acknowledging thoughts with the proper labels such as, "Blaming Ted for my anger," or "Worrying," or "Sad feeling," it will be easy to see them. Notice how they pull you away from the current moment. Note how much stress and unhappiness they are causing you. And discover how they lose their power over you as you remain living in the here and now, stress-free, happy and content.

CHAPTER 5

THE POWER TO CONTROL HOW YOU FEEL

Living in the moment is a simple concept. Let go of your thoughts and live in the here and now. But when put into practice, it can be somewhat challenging. The reason for this is because our minds are conditioned to act or react a certain way. It is all we know. It is our comfort zone. And we are very protective of it. We are afraid of losing control, unless we have chosen to do so with drugs or alcohol.

As children, we live in the current moment, eager to learn and explore our world. But our parents, teachers, relatives and friends taught us the only way they knew how. It was the wrong way. As we grew up, we learned more and more to remember things and to dream about the future. I am not talking about remembering things we learned but remembering all of our experiences. We kept seeking pleasures of the senses to make ourselves happy.

When we found something we liked, we clung to it, trying to retain the happiness. When the happiness faded, we wanted to get it back so we repeated whatever it was that we liked, again and again. So we conditioned our brains to believe that pleasure means happiness. But it was never enough to quench all the craving and desire.

Now we are trying to dismantle that belief system to get to the core of ourselves, which basks in the bliss of unconditional happiness. It is there all the time. We do not have to buy something or go some place or eat something to create happiness. It is simply a matter of breaking a bad habit. Again, I want to stress that we are not trying to eliminate all of our memory of the past or prevent thinking about the future. We are simply identifying those thoughts and when they are harmful, causing stress and unhappiness.

With Thought Watching, you are creating a new habit. I urge you to resist the tendency to create your own method. The false you is going to constantly tell you that you are smarter than me and if you just change such and such, you will get to the goal faster and easier. In the early stages of your practice, the false you seems to be fighting against revealing the true you. It is primarily due to being fearful of stepping out of your comfort zone.

Remember to just "observe" those thoughts and feelings. Eventually the false you will surrender and awaken to the truth.

The human mind follows a specific seven stage pattern, regardless of who you are or what you know. Each stage takes a fraction of a second. The progression of each stage is dependent on the previous stage. You would never get to the second stage or beyond, if you didn't have "contact" (Stage 1) in the first place. The same holds true if you stop it at any stage along the way. The progression stops. And that is exactly what you are going to learn to do, because the final stage is stress and unhappiness, which is what you currently have, when it is left alone and free to follow its habitual pattern.

7 STAGE THOUGHT PATTERN

STAGE 1 – CONTACT: There is contact between an object and one of your senses, sight, sound, smell, taste, touch or mind which creates a thought. Note that mind is included with your five senses, which represents thoughts that trigger thoughts.

STAGE 2 – THOUGHT CATEGORIZED: The thought gets categorized as good, bad or neutral. If it is neutral, the pattern will usually stop right there.

This stage can also be referred to as part of your perception. Perception consists of naming and identifying the object and how you feel about it. Even if it is a new object, being experienced for the first time, it may be similar or remind you of another object and may initially get the wrong categorization. So thoughts categorized as good or bad allow the progression of the stages.

STAGE 3 – FEELING: The thought becomes a feeling or emotion of happy, mad, sad or fearful. This stage is where you want to stop. This stage is still in the current moment. All the stages preceding this are pulling you away from the current moment.

STAGE 4 – CRAVING & DESIRE: The feeling or emotion leads to craving and desire. Craving for more of that feeling or emotion to continue or desire for it to end. This stage is where the seed of stress gets planted.

STAGE 5 – CLINGING: The craving and desire leads to clinging, which is trying to hold onto good or bad feelings. When we cling to bad feelings, it is not because we want to continue feeling bad. We cling to them because we think it will make us feel better. This clinging stage can lead us to believe that we are in a good or bad mood, which is because we have grouped several incidents of good or bad feelings together.

STAGE 6 – BECOMING: Clinging leads to becoming, which is becoming a different state of mind or appearance. We are clinging to hopes of becoming happy.

STAGE 7 – STRESS: Becoming leads to stress which is also known as anxiety, worry, fear, sadness, anger, despair, hatred and a long list of negative states of mind. It opens the door for additional thoughts to go right to the fourth stage of craving and desire, and then continue in the same pattern. You are now outside of the here and now and have a difficult time getting back.

Your Thought Watching training is preparing you to be able to see the pattern developing and prevent it from ever going beyond the third stage, which leaves you in the true you state of stress-free happiness. When you perform the third step of "let it go," you are letting go of the possibility of progression to stages four and beyond, which ultimately ends in stress and unhappiness.

Let's take a closer look at what you are giving up when you let go of thoughts and feelings and stop the seven stage thought pattern from progressing.

Craving and desire (Stage 4): This is the bait and hook. Based on the feeling you got, you would crave it if it was good or desire that it will end if it was bad. Both have negative consequences. Craving and desire for an object or person is a set up for disappointment, because it is conditional happiness. If the conditions do not meet your expectations, you get disappointed. All conditional happiness fades away and ends.

You might also have a certain amount of time that you want the happy feeling to last or how strong it should be, and that will usually guarantee disappointment. Or you are craving for something you can not get, or may never get. Craving for a bad feeling to end creates frustration and anger which usually triggers additional negative thoughts. This continues until you find a way to interrupt the pattern.

All that you need to do is simply enjoy the moment when it is happening and nothing more. So it is pure enjoyment and no disappointment. When the true you becomes more apparent, you will discover that you do not have to crave external sources of happiness. You will be happy and content all of the time.

Whenever you have advanced to the fourth stage of

craving and desire, it usually means that you are taking ownership of your thoughts and feelings. Taking ownership is when you think in terms of me, mine, my or I to thoughts as your own. Thoughts like, "I feel so bad about that," or "That makes me mad," or, "I wish I could be happy for once." When you take ownership of thoughts in this way, you are granting permission for the seven stage pattern to progress, which ultimately ends in a negative state of mind.

Here is an example of taking ownership: You are on a diet and you see one of your favorite treats – a chocolate cupcake. Then you instantly get a thought like, "Mmmm, that sure looks good." What you should do is acknowledge it by saying, "Craving and desire," and let it go. If you decide to take ownership of that thought by saying, "I really want that. That's my favorite," you will generate a whole string of thoughts like, "One little cupcake isn't going to hurt. I've been really good. I even had a lighter breakfast than usual today. That's really going to taste great. I love chocolate. I want it. I'm having it." So you go ahead and eat it. The result is, yes, it tasted great, but then you felt guilty for having it and you get disappointed in your lack of will power. Not to mention that you delayed losing weight a little bit more.

What is it that you really want when you crave or desire for something? Isn't it ultimately, to achieve the happy feeling that you get from it? The problem is, that is conditional happiness. All conditional happiness is impermanent. Unconditional happiness is what you have right here and now. That doesn't fade away. What makes it appear as if it is fading away, is when you start craving for something, thereby giving it up, and you unknowingly replace it with conditional happiness.

Clinging (Stage 5): If you have allowed craving and desire, then clinging will usually follow. If it was something good, you try to hold onto the feeling. Like when you get together with people and laugh and joke. It feels good so you do all that you can to cling to the feeling and keep the laughing and joking continuing. If it was bad, you might cling to it in an effort to make yourself feel better. For example: If you were mad at someone, you might get a thought like, "He made me so mad," followed by, "He was so mean and rotten. I shouldn't be treated like that. It's not fair that I have to be this upset." A much better way would be immediately following the thought, "He made me so mad," you would acknowledge it by saying, "angry feeling," then let it go. You cut off the pattern at Stage 3 FEELING. Do you see how you can take control of the way you think and feel? You are not ruled by emotion.

This is a good time to mention about your interaction with other people. Most people say, "She made me mad," or, "He hurt my feelings," or, "They made me feel like an outcast." The truth is, no one can make you feel a certain way. I repeat, no one can make you feel a certain way. They can say something that might trigger a bad feeling, but ultimately, you are responsible for how you feel. That means, if you do not want to feel bad, you can choose not to.

If I mailed you a package and you told the delivery man that you are refusing it, who does the package belong to? Right, it still belongs to me. In the same way, if someone says something hurtful to you and you refuse to accept it, their words still belong to him or her. If you blame others for the way you feel, you have to wait for them to fix it, or else you will carry a lot of animosity around with you. Animosity is based on feelings from the past. That takes you away from the here and now and you carry stress around with you.

Any time that you cling to your thoughts or feelings, you are not allowing closure and you are inviting stress and unhappiness. Clinging also takes you out of the here and now. Since our mind and bodies are in a constant state of change, when we try to hold onto something, it is very stressful. It is like trying to paddle a rubber raft, on a raging river, to try and hold it still. The only thing that is constant is the true you.

Often, you will be totally convinced that you need to hold onto thoughts. Sometimes, you will even come up with excuses of why you should cling to them, such as, "I need to figure this out," or, "I need to come to terms with this," or, "I don't know if I'm ever going to forgive her for this." Or you might think, "If I just let it go, I'm saying that it's okay that he hurt me and it's my fault." But who pays the price when you cling? You do! You have a lot more power over your thoughts than the false you thinks. Let it go! Clinging equals pain and suffering. Every little thing that you cling to means that you are carrying around more stress. This becomes increasingly more apparent, the more you let go.

There's an awful lot going on, subconsciously, wouldn't you agree? When one learns to be an auto mechanic, he must understand what each and every part does to contribute to a successfully running engine. In the same way, you must understand what each thought is doing to contribute to the result. Thought Watching and Breath Watching will reveal the pattern to you and you will understand it inside and out. It is not a matter of studying a whole bunch of information and trying to learn it and remember it, like you did in school the night before a test. This is much much easier! Just observe.

From contact as a requisite condition comes feeling. From feeling as a requisite condition comes craving. From craving as a requisite condition comes clinging. From clinging as a requisite condition comes becoming.

From contact as a requisite condition comes feeling. Thus it has been said. And this is the way to understand how from contact as a requisite condition comes feeling. If there were no contact at all, in any way, of anything anywhere i.e., contact at the eye, contact at the ear, contact at the nose, contact at the tongue, contact at the body, or contact at the intellect in the utter absence of contact, from the cessation of contact, would feeling be discerned?"

"No, lord."

"Thus this is a cause, this is a reason, this is an origination, this is a requisite condition for feeling, i.e., contact."

5 THE POWER TO CONTROL HOW YOU FEEL

"From feeling as a requisite condition comes craving. Thus it has been said. And this is the way to understand how from feeling as a requisite condition comes craving. If there were no feeling at all, in any way, of anything anywhere — i.e., feeling born of contact at the eye, feeling born of contact at the ear, feeling born of contact at the nose, feeling born of contact at the tongue, feeling born of contact at the body, or feeling born of contact at the intellect — in the utter absence of feeling, from the cessation of feeling, would craving be discerned?"

"No, lord."

"Thus this is a cause, this is a reason, this is an origination, this is a requisite condition for craving, i.e., feeling."

"From craving as a requisite condition comes clinging. Thus it has been said. And this is the way to understand how from craving as a requisite condition comes clinging. If there were no craving at all, in any way, of anything anywhere — i.e., craving for sensuality, craving for becoming, craving for no becoming — in the utter absence of craving, from the cessation of craving, would clinging be discerned?"

5 THE POWER TO CONTROL HOW YOU FEEL

"No, lord."

"Thus this is a cause, this is a reason, this is an origination, this is a requisite condition for clinging, i.e., craving."

"From clinging as a requisite condition comes becoming. Thus it has been said. And this is the way to understand how from clinging as a requisite condition comes becoming. If there were no clinging at all, in any way, of anything anywhere i.e., clinging to sensuality, clinging to precepts and practices, clinging to views, or clinging to doctrines of the self in the utter absence of clinging, from the cessation of clinging, would becoming be discerned?"

"No, lord."

"Thus this is a cause, this is a reason, this is an origination, this is a requisite condition for becoming, i.e., clinging."
-BUDDHIST SCRIPTURES

CHAPTER 6

BREAKING BAD HABITS

Old and bad habits are hard to break, aren't they? Let's take a look at some of the fears that you might encounter when you try to break those habits and let go.

FEAR OF LOSING CONTROL: Fear itself, is part of the false you. It is based on your prediction of the future, which is not in the here and now. You can not control the future any better by worrying about it, or being fearful of it. By letting go of that fear, you stay in the present moment, clear minded and brave. Any thoughts that you let go of are replaced by their opposite. Let go of fear and bravery takes its place. You are going to be much more in control of yourself without the fear.

FEAR OF LOSING PLEASANT MEMORIES: Your memory is going to greatly improve, the more you let go of thoughts. You do not lose or give up your memories. You are able to enjoy them much more when you are not clinging to them and trying to manipulate them.

FEAR OF BECOMING AN EMPTY SHELL WITHOUT EMOTIONS: Do not worry. You will still be yourself, only better. You will still have emotions, but they are completely different when you are not clinging to them. It simply ensures that mad, sad and fearful emotions do not overstay their welcome.

FEAR THAT YOU WILL NOT REMEMBER THINGS YOU HAVE TO DO: You will be amazed how much your memory will dramatically improve when your mind is cleared of all the stress you are hanging on to, and all the stress you are constantly manufacturing.

FEAR OF BEING A DOORMAT FOR PEOPLE TO WALK ALL OVER YOU: By letting go of hatred and anger, puts you in a better position to deal with mean or abusive people. Do you want to "act," or would you rather just "react?" When you get to know how damaging it has been clinging to hatred and anger, you will become much more sympathetic and compassionate toward other people who are still trapped in that cycle.

All of these fears are completely unjustified. Do not predict the future in a negative way. If you are struggling with any of these fears, then you are clinging. Observe, acknowledge and let it go. Have I been anything less than one hundred percent truthful? I have lived through all of these fears already for you. I am saving you from wasting your time and helping you discover the true you quickly and efficiently.

To understand where all of these fears come from, you have to realize that all your knowledge and experience is what you are relying on for reference. It is like having an outdated computer that you are trying to run new software on. You are coming into new, uncharted territory with what you are learning now, and that is like your new software. But you do not want to use it on your old mind, which is like an outdated computer. If you do, you create preconceived notions of what to expect. That translates into slower learning of new material. What can you do to prevent this? Observe then acknowledge, "Preconceived notion," and let it go. Three simple steps, yet so difficult for a cluttered mind. Observe, acknowledge, let it go.

A cluttered mind means a whole lot of stress! All of the fears, preconceived notions, hatred, ego, negative predictions of the future, etc. causes you to carry around unnecessary self-imposed stress. Let it go, let it go, let it go, and watch your stress melt away!

6 BREAKING BAD HABITS

People have a lot of habitual patterns of behavior. Like living outside of the here and now. We have gotten used to a lot of mental stimulation and the present moment can seem boring at times. Or we are trying to avoid problems or stressful situations. The very act of trying to avoid it, is the reason it is a problem or stressful. When you hold onto a problem and another problem comes up, then you have two problems. If you try to solve them, you can only give partial effort to each one, because you have the other one floating around in your mind also. More stress is created and frustration and anger sets in.

Add to that, all the thoughts that you are clinging to, and sooner or later, you explode with sadness or anger. So then you decide that it is best to let go of something or else you will explode again. A short time later, you repeat this pattern of behavior. Why do you do that? Because you did not know of a better way. You did not have a choice. Now you do. Observe, acknowledge and let it go!

The current moment is perfect. It does not have to live up to certain expectations. It certainly can not be regretful. It does not age and it does not die because it changes faster than you can say what it is doing. It is supreme bliss, nirvana, enlightenment. It does not belong to you and it does not belong to me. It is completely free. Free to be slow, fast, high, low, happy, sad, forward, backward, wet, dry or boring. The current moment does not know where it is going and does not care where it has been. It is peace, love, tranquility. It is without limitations. There are no rules. It is you. The true you.

When you abandon the false you and reveal the true you, there is no such thing as a problem. There is no such thing as boredom. There is nothing to fear or avoid. There is no stress, jealousy, no anger, no depression. It is completely liberating! You can achieve it! I have given you the method to achieve it. If it is not worth the effort and you want to continue chasing happiness and being stressed out, then say goodbye right now. But if stress-free unconditional happiness is worth a little effort, then observe, acknowledge, let it go.

The chains of habit are too weak to be felt until they are too strong to be broken.
-Samuel Johnson

Some rules are nothing but old habits that people are afraid to change.
-Therese Anne Fowler

6 BREAKING BAD HABITS

Everything you are used to, once done long enough, starts to seem natural, even though it might not be.
-Julien Smith

Bad habits are like chains that are too light to feel until they are too heavy to carry.
-Warren Buffet

Habit is habit and not to be flung out of the window by any man, but coaxed downstairs a step at a time.
-Mark Twain

I recommend that you bookmark this page and let two entire days pass before you continue with the next chapter. Try to resist the desire to look at the next chapter to see what it is about. Observe and Acknowledge "Desire" and Let it go... and bookmark this page.

CHAPTER 7

HOW TO SIMPLIFY YOUR COMPLICATED MIND

The world is full of chaos and confusion. But we get ourselves into the mindset that everything has to run perfectly, just like we predict and would like it to be. We want to make plans, staying optimistic, but what happens when something goes wrong? What happens if it turns out different than we had planned?

When was the last time that you said, "I can't wait to go on vacation and get sick!" or "This new restaurant is going to have cold, disgusting food." or "The house next door just sold and I bet the new neighbors will be completely unsociable." These statements may be a little extreme, but these kinds of predictions would probably work out better than if you were completely upbeat and positive. Why? Because they leave no room for disappointment.

All too often, we are completely unable to accept

anything that makes us sad, angry or stressful, after we have planned or predicted the perfect future. If we accept the fact that things can go wrong, and accept the fact that it is an imperfect world, then there is no disappointment. Everything is perfect just like it is.

Don't get me wrong. I am not saying that you should not be optimistic. I am just trying to help you see how you should not expect perfection for those times when you do have to plan for something in the future. It is far better to be optimistic in the current moment.

Take the weather as an example. Sometimes it is completely unpredictable. Sometimes the experts predict sunshine and it gets cloudy or rains. Either way, you get what you get. It is what it is. It will not change no matter how upset that you get over it. It will not always turn out like you thought or wanted it to. So bring an umbrella just in case.

It is exactly the same way with anything in the future. It is unpredictable. You get what you get. If you have to plan something for the future, then do so with the knowledge that it could be less than perfect. The reason that people buy insurance is for that very reason, that something could go wrong.

7 HOW TO SIMPLIFY YOUR COMPLICATED MIND

You do not have to be optimistic to buy insurance. You do not have to be pessimistic. You are just prepared for any way that it might turn out. That is how you should treat all plans for the future.

If you have progressed enough, you will have noticed that you are both, more than you thought you were, and less than you thought that you were. You are constantly in a state of change.

A lot of stress comes from trying to hold on to what you think that you are. Let's say that you think that you are brave. And you may be completely right about that. But suppose that something just happened and you discovered that you were not brave at all. If you had been clinging to the thought that you are brave and then you aren't, there is a major clash, resulting in disappointment in yourself and stress. Now, multiply that by the number of characteristics that you think you are and you can imagine how much clashing, disappointment, frustration and stress there is going on all the time.

Every part of your body and every part of your mind is constantly in a state of change. Have you ever noticed your memory of a certain past event changes over time? What about your likes and dislikes? They've changed too, right? You are constantly changing. It is scary but true. Nobody wants to face that fact. And I'm sorry I just hit you over the head with it. We want so much, to be in control of ourselves at all times. But if you are brave enough to accept the fact that you are changing constantly, you will relieve yourself of a whole lot of stress. You have no control over it anyhow. The more skilled that you are at living in the current moment, the more accepting you will become.

Just a drop of water in an endless sea. All we do crumbles to the ground though we refuse to see. Dust in the wind. All we are is dust in the wind.
-Song by Kansas : Dust in the Wind

Most people are very preoccupied with their appearance. They do not want to look older. That is thinking about the future. And they wish that they looked like they did when they were younger. That is thinking about the past. But right here in the current moment, they are perfect as they are. If they only knew it.

Then we have another factor to consider. No part of you exists on its own. Every part of you is dependent on something else. You are made up of the four elements of earth, water, heat and wind, just like the rest of the universe. You do not have a self nature nor does anything in the universe have a self nature. Plants need earth, water and sunshine. People need water, air and warmth.

So what does all of this mean in terms of your existence? When you merge with the universe and all of its inhabitants, you let go of a giant struggle that you did not even know that you were having. You realize that you do not have to worry so much if you have a problem. It is going to change. It is going to rain and the sun is going to shine. You are going to have bad times and you are going to have good times. But you can't have one without the other. Without the bad, you wouldn't know what good is. Soon, you will stop categorizing everything as one or the other.

Peacefulness will envelop you when you come to terms with this. You do not have to struggle or cling to existence, or try to control everything. When you learn to let go of trying to control everything, you actually gain more control. Not more control over events but control over yourself. Remember that clinging means stress because it pulls you away from the stress-free current moment.

7 HOW TO SIMPLIFY YOUR COMPLICATED MIND

Even your relationship with the world is not as it appears. Everything that you experience through your senses is dependent on several things. Objects only exist in dependence of the mind labeling them, in dependence of their collection of parts, and in dependence of their causes and conditions. When you are viewing objects as completely separate, with their own self nature, then you will have likes and dislikes. That means clinging.

The same is true when you see yourself as separate, with your own self nature, you are clinging. I know, I'm getting really deep, not to give you more to try and understand but to show you that much of reality is an illusion and the more we try to separate and control things, the more stress and unhappiness we have.

We have somehow evolved into very complicated humans. Does life really have to be so complex? A mirage in the desert can have a person completely convinced that he or she sees water, only to find out that it does not exist. In the same way, our minds can have us completely convinced that things are a certain way, but on closer examination, we find out that we have been fooled. So we unknowingly buy into our beliefs about something, that may not even exist. We cling to our beliefs and they help form an ego. The ego helps to convince us that we exist and builds a world around us. That is how we create our comfort zone. Our beliefs, our ego, our world.

When we are unwillingly pulled out of our comfort zone, we have a lot of stress and anxiety. An extreme case would be a panic attack. Fear is born when we worry about being pulled out of our comfort zone. It is for that very reason, that our minds are enslaved to an endless cycle of comfort and fear. Together with that, is an endless cycle of peace and stress, pleasure and pain. So if we remove fear, we free our minds from the cycle.

Do you see where fear is being born and nurtured in your own life? What is it that pulls you out of your comfort zone? Am I doing that to you now? The only reason that fear exists is because you have a comfort zone in the first place. How ironic is that? You have fear because you have comfort. Every time that you have fear, you cling to your comfort zone and that reinforces your belief that you need to have a comfort zone.

But that is just like a mirage. When you let go of your comfort zone, and step out into that scary world, you stop the cycle and free your mind. When your mind is free, it opens to the truth and you see that you have been fooled. When you no longer have a comfort zone, you no longer have the fear of leaving it. You no longer have fear. Without fear, you no longer have stress. There is absolutely no fear in the current moment. Whenever you feel fearful, it is based on past memories or future predictions.

You cannot just instantly dismantle your belief system. You cannot instantly drop your comfort zone. Why not? Because of your fear. And because you are subconsciously convinced that you need it. You are also certain that if you do not have your comfort zone, you will be scared to death. All of that fear means stress and that prevents you from being able to change.

Whenever you feel fearful, just remember that it is temporary. The more you are able to let go, the less fear you will have. It will eventually fade away, never to return again. Everything is temporary. Every thought is temporary. Every feeling is temporary. The way that you look is temporary. Your views and opinions are temporary. Your health is temporary. Your life is temporary. So why do we try to make everything permanent? In a word, fear.

Observe when you are fearful. Acknowledge it by

saying, "Fearful feeling," and let it go. Remember not to take ownership of the fear. You do not want to acknowledge it by saying, "I'm scared," "I'm afraid," or "I'm fearful."

CHAPTER 8
REMOVING SELF IMPOSED OBSTACLES

Most people have self imposed obstacles that are keeping them locked in a world of stress and suffering. Following are some of the major obstacles that you will probably need a little extra effort to eradicate.

SENSUAL DESIRE: Lust, fantasizing and craving will keep the art of clinging strong and letting go of thoughts nearly impossible. I am not talking about everyday passion or love here, but rather, the strong attachment to craving and desire. It usually stems from the constant need to generate good feelings, both physically and mentally. Fire eventually burns out and you will no longer stoke the flame when you develop unconditional happiness. All of that lust and fantasizing is dreaming of the future and that is where anger, fear and sadness resides.

HATRED: This is merely an excuse for clinging to negative thoughts. Like I said before, it is not that you want to retain negative thoughts, you think it is helping you feel better. Your hatred toward people makes you feel bad, so you try to make yourself feel better by blaming someone for making you feel that way. The truth is, that it is the hatred itself, that negative emotion, that is making you feel bad. Anger is outside of the here and now. That negative emotion means stress.

Let go of hatred and free your mind of unnecessary stress. Forgive and forget is a common phrase offering great advice. Forgive people for being less than perfect. People make mistakes. How would you feel if other people hated you? A lot of hatred toward other people stems from hatred toward yourself. Then there is hatred toward objects or events. You know, all those times that you say, "I hate that." Even if it is just a few things that you hate, it means stress. Hatred pulls you out of the current moment. Observe it, acknowledge it by saying, "Hatred" or "Angry feeling," and let it go!

LAZINESS: I am referring to mental laziness, not being physically lazy or tired. There are times when you are too lazy to practice Thought Watching or have a Breath Watching session. You consider it too much effort without immediate reward. You must force yourself to press forward and stay ener-gized and focused or you will fall victim to letting your mind control you, the way it has your entire life. Remember that, over the years, your mind has found ways to feel calm and relaxed (conditional happiness) and those automatic habitual patterns need to be changed. You need to keep going. Practice Thought Watching, every moment of every day. Once the initial thrill has faded away, because you still have conditional happiness, you may begin to feel like it is a chore to continue. If so, you are being fooled by the false you.

DOUBT: Whether you have doubt in yourself, doubt in my teaching, doubt about others or any other doubt or uncertainty, it is one of the biggest hurdles to overcome. Recognize when you have doubt and acknowledge it by saying, "There is doubt," and let it go. Your doubts will be replaced with conviction, regarding my teaching. Nothing I have taught you needs to be accepted on pure faith. You should only believe it when you have person-ally experienced it. It is through your own discern-ment that your mind will comfortably accept it. As for the doubt in yourself, try to focus on your posit-ive qualities. Do not beat yourself up. Doubt is nothing more than a negative prediction of the future. Doubt eventually breaks down by itself, replaced with conviction, but you can help it along.

8 REMOVING SELF IMPOSED OBSTACLES

Make an ongoing conscious effort to recognize all of these self imposed obstacles and be aware of how much stress they create. When you subconsciously associate these hindrances with negative states of mind, that pull you away from the current moment, they will start to weaken.

There are five impediments and hindrances of the mind that stultify insight. What five?

Sensual desire is an impediment and hindrance of the mind that stultifies insight. Ill-will... Sloth and torpor... Restlessness and remorse... Skeptical doubt are impediments and hindrances of the mind that stultify insight.

Without having overcome these five, it is impossible for a monk whose insight thus lacks strength and power, to know his own true good, the good of others, and the good of both; nor will he be capable of realizing that super-human state of distinctive achievement, the knowledge and vision enabling the attainment of sanctity.

But if a monk has overcome these five impediments and hindrances of the mind that stultify insight, then it is possible that, with his strong insight, he can know his own true good, the good of others, and the good of both; and he will be capable of realizing that superhuman state of distinctive achievement, the knowledge and vision enabling the attainment of sanctity.

How does a monk practice mind-object contemplation on the mental objects of the five hindrances?

Herein, monks, when sensual desire is present in him the monk knows, "There is sensual desire in me," or when sensual desire is absent he knows, "There is no sensual desire in me." He knows how the arising of non-arisen sensual desire comes to be; he knows how the rejection of the arisen sensual desire comes to be; and he knows how the non-arising in the future of the rejected sensual desire comes to be.

When ill-will is present in him, the monk knows, "There is ill-will in me," or when ill-will is absent he knows, "There is no ill-will in me." He knows how the arising of non-arisen ill-will comes to be; he knows how the rejection of the arisen ill-will comes to be; and he knows how the non-arising in the future of the rejected ill-will comes to be.

8 REMOVING SELF IMPOSED OBSTACLES

When sloth and torpor are present in him, the monk knows, "There is sloth and torpor in me," or when sloth and torpor are absent he knows, "There is no sloth and torpor in me." He knows how the arising of non-arisen sloth and torpor comes to be; he knows how the rejection of the arisen sloth and torpor comes to be; and he knows how the non-arising in the future of the rejected sloth and torpor comes to be.

When restlessness and remorse are present in him, the monk knows, "There are restlessness and remorse in me," or when agitation and remorse are absent he knows, "There are no restlessness and remorse in me." He knows how the arising of non-arisen restlessness and remorse comes to be; he knows how the rejection of the arisen restlessness and remorse comes to be; and he knows how the non-arising in the future of the rejected restlessness and remorse comes to be.

When skeptical doubt is present in him, the monk knows, "There is skeptical doubt in me," or when skeptical doubt is absent he knows, "There is no skeptical doubt in me." He knows how the arising of non-arisen skeptical doubt comes to be; he knows how the rejection of the arisen skeptical doubt comes to be; and he

knows how the non-arising in the future of the rejected skeptical doubt comes to be.
-BUDDHIST SCRIPTURES

Another type of obstacle is clinging. All of the clinging that you do keeps your mind tied to its mental process and repeating the same patterns of behavior. These behaviors have been repeated over and over, year after year. For most people, it is very challenging to change them. See if you are clinging to any of the following.

CLINGING TO RULES, VIEWS, BELIEFS AND OPINIONS: This type of clinging is usually done subconsciously, as a defense mechanism. Defending your comfort zone and what defines you as an individual. You get upset with anyone who tries to change your mind over to their way of thinking.

Here is an example of clinging to rules: Lets say that you like to do things in an orderly fashion. If you go to a shopping mall for the first time, your rule is to start on the level that you come in on and you go to the right. Then you continue all the way around until you have come full circle back to where you started from. Then you go to another level and you do the same routine. This is your rule of how to be orderly and efficient, so you are sure to see every store in the mall. You consider this the right way, and that everyone else should do it this way. But today, you are joined by a friend who spots a store on the other side of the mall, as soon as you walked in, and wants to go there first. But you were all set to go to the right. You consider the new plan to be completely out of order and you are instantly agitated. It is not the proper way as far as you are concerned. You are clinging to your rule that you should be going in an orderly fashion, to the right. This is the birth of stress.

Another example would be, that you believe that when you go to a fast food restaurant, and there are two lines of people waiting, you should stand in the middle so you can go to which ever line moves ahead first. You consider this to be the fairest way. But someone behind you feels differently and asks, with a little attitude, which line you are in. That is stress.

If you are plagued by this type of clinging, let it go. You are trying to detach from anything that causes stress. Observe, acknowledge, let it go.

CLINGING TO YOUR BODY: You are constantly concerned about how you look and what you can do to look better. You wish that you could look like so and so. You are very concerned about what others will think of you.   This sort of clinging also includes constant comparison of how you looked before, when you were younger, or happier or more energetic.

You are convinced that looking good makes you happy. So you cling to all of your bodily imperfections. That scar, big chin, crooked nose, poor complexion, fat face, big gut, wide butt, one leg shorter than the other, or whatever else is less than perfect. Think about how much stress is involved with never being satisfied.   Here is yet another example of craving and desire.

Let go of your view of yourself, and how you think you would rather look, and you will let go of stress. Do you think you could announce to the world that you have all kinds of faults? Can you expose all of your imperfections for all to see? That is where you need to be. You need to be able to say, "I am full of imperfections, mentally and physically.   I am human. I have faults. I make mistakes. I do not have to live up to my own or any other person's expectations."

CLINGING TO YOUR PERCEPTIONS: How you interpret what you take in through your senses becomes your sense of comfort and you cling to it. You classify everything as either good or bad, with no in between. You try your hardest to manipulate reality to suit your needs. This type of clinging becomes a huge problem when a certain reality can not be altered. Clinging to perceptions keeps you locked into your belief system which is often self destructive. Be aware of your perceptions and work toward seeing things as they are, not as you want them to be.

Keep in mind that your belief system is constantly in a state of change anyhow, so disallowing change means that you are clinging and clinging means stress.

CLINGING TO YOUR FEELINGS: This is when you are constantly trying to hold onto good feelings and repel bad feelings. You are always looking for pleasure of your senses. Everything is unsatisfactory. It is never good enough. Feelings come and go, all the time, so you cannot hold onto them. Even when you try loading yourself up with new, good feelings, those fade away also.

It is time to get off of the treadmill and accept the fact that feelings come and go. Remember to continue your role as observer rather than reactor. If you do not entertain the feelings, they will not control you, and grow cold right there. It is like a growing plant. Deprive it of water and it stops growing. Have faith, for now, which will soon be replaced with conviction, that you will feel good without holding on.

"And what is clinging? What is the origination of clinging? What is the cessation of clinging? What is the way of practice leading to the cessation of clinging?

"There are these four types of clinging: sensuality clinging, view clinging, precept & practice clinging, and doctrine of self clinging. This is called clinging.

"From the origination of craving comes the origination of clinging. From the cessation of craving comes the cessation of clinging. And the way of practice leading to the cessation of clinging is just this very noble eightfold path: right view, right resolve, right speech, right action, right livelihood, right effort, right mindfulness, right concentration.

"Now, when a disciple of the noble ones discerns clinging, the origination of clinging, the cessation of clinging, and the way of practice leading to the cessation of clinging in this way, when — having entirely abandoned passion-obsession, having abolished aversion-ob-

session, having uprooted the view-&-conceit obsession 'I am'; having abandoned ignorance & given rise to clear knowing — he has put an end to suffering & stress right in the here-&-now, it is to this extent, too, that a disciple of the noble ones is a person of right view... who has arrived at this true Dhamma."
-BUDDHIST SCRIPTURES

I must congratulate you on your dedication to changing yourself, but I must warn you. You may find yourself trying to change your friends and family as well. You will probably begin to see how much other people are needlessly suffering. You will notice how they are doing all the wrong things that keep them locked in a world of stress and suffering. With your new found skills, you may wish to throw a lifeline to those in need. If I can make a recommendation, DO NOT DO IT. Do not try to help anyone. Not to be selfish, but to save yourself from additional stress.

People do not want help unless they go looking for it, in a proactive role. Otherwise, you will be taking away their comfort zone. Even if that comfort is making them miserable. They are comfortable because they know exactly what they are dealing with. What you are proposing may instantly spark fear of the unknown. They may also feel that you are exposing their faults for the world to see.

If someone should ask you about it, by all means, you should share it. But share it in such a way that you are referring to yourself and what it is doing for you, not what it will do for them. Do this by saying, "It has helped me" rather than "It will help you." They will be much more receptive that way. Or you can simply refer them to this book. Remember that you were introduced to this knowledge slowly and methodically. Without even trying, people around you will benefit from your relaxed and happy demeanor.

Just the mere fact that you are noticing other people's faults will be educational and of great benefit to you. It may seem selfish and conceited, but while you are still in training, it is all about you!

Chances are good that you will not get sick as often. Stress depletes your body's vitamin C, thus lowering your resistance to germs. So, not only will you feel good mentally, but you will feel better physically as well.

Continue to diligently practice Thought Watching and Breath Watching which are key to changing your mind's conditioned pattern of behavior. You will know when you have changed and will no longer require practicing.

From time to time, you may experience setbacks. You are as high as a kite and think that you have attained a certain level and suddenly find that you have crashed and burned.

What is happening is, you have been getting happier and lowering your stress more and more. You get all glossy eyed and mystical with a constant smile on your face. Much like a "born again" religious person. This is a fabricated state of mind and subject to cessation, sooner or later. It seduces you into believing that you have made permanent changes. It is the false you. Remember that you are conditioned to cling to pleasure of the senses, which includes the intellect.

Regardless of how well that you have progressed, and how stress-free and happy that you are, you still have to let it go. True, unconditional happiness will stay, even when you let it go. It is not actually that you are letting go of it, you are just not clinging to it. That is the most subtle difference that is hard for the mind to accept – that it could be as easy as letting go of happiness to retain happiness. What is easy to remember is that you should not cling to feelings, whether they are good, bad or anything in between.

When you find yourself clinging to the new you, just remember to observe, acknowledge, let it go. It is very possible that this entire scenario will play out over and over. You will know when the true you has finally emerged. One of the sure signs is when you no longer have the need or desire to hold onto happiness. It will happen for you if you observe, acknowledge and let it go.

CHAPTER 9

ENDING YOUR ADDICTIONS

This chapter is about ending addictions to drugs, alcohol, food, sex, gambling, tobacco, etc. It is solely concerning the psychological rather than the physical aspects of addiction. I am not a medical doctor and not qualified by any means to comment about any physical addiction that may occur. The following information is solely my personal opinion and advice and is not intended to replace possible medication or professional help that you may require.

I believe that the better part of addiction is psychological rather than physical. I have personally triumphed over addictions to cigarettes and drugs, by psychological methods so I speak from experience to that extent.

Addictions are ultimately addictions to the good feeling that you get. You crave more and more good feelings by continuing to do what you do. The

7 Stage Thought Pattern outlined in Chapter 5 looks like this:

Contact > Thought Categorized > Feeling > Craving & Desire > Clinging > Becoming > Stress

This is how that pattern plays out. Let's say that you are addicted to drugs. Prior to doing drugs, you are getting thoughts (Contact) of feeling good (Thought Categorized) which you associate with the use of the drug. That good feeling (Feeling) leads to wanting more good feelings (Craving & Desire) which leads to strong attachment to that activity (Clinging). That clinging is the addiction. Clinging is your instructions of how to be happy, even if it is only temporary (Becoming). That whole pattern ends with sadness, disappointment and despair (Stress) when you realize the good feeling doesn't and can not last. So it loops right back to the thought of doing it again to get the good feeling.

The way to stop the addiction is to stop the pattern from going beyond "feeling." Which brings us back to the concept of living in the moment. Craving for more of a good feeling is based on thoughts toward the future of obtaining that good feeling, based on memories of the past of what that good feeling actually feels like. Eliminate the past and the future and it is perfect the way you feel right in this very moment.

Craving & desire must be brought to an end in order to end the addiction. The way to end that craving and desire is to stop the pattern. The way to stop the pattern is to understand the pattern. The way to understand the pattern is to observe it. The way to observe it is applying the exercise of Thought Watching. The goal of Thought Watching is to gain control of what causes stress and unhappiness and stop it from developing once it is born at the "contact" stage.

Contact begins at any of your senses of sight, sound, smell, taste, touch or mind which creates a thought. So if it is food that you are addicted to, the 7 Stage Thought Pattern could begin if you taste or smell something. If you are addicted to gambling, the sights and sounds at a casino could trigger the pattern.

In summary, you will be able to terminate any unwanted addictions that you may have when you have discovered the true you and enlightenment. In the mean time, a strong conscious effort to keep focused on the current moment will help you if you are trying to beat an addiction.

CHAPTER 10

KARMA CONNECTING YOUR PAST TO YOUR FUTURE

I want to talk to you a little about karma. Most people have heard of this word used in conjunction with "bad" like "bad karma." Bad karma is a term that many people think that it is the same as bad luck. That is completely inaccurate.

Karma, which can be good or bad, is just like an echo. Whatever you send out in words or deeds, will find its way back to you. When you send out good, you will get good back. When you send out bad, you will get bad back. Sometimes it is immediate and sometimes, it does not come back for a very long time.

There is a connection, here in the present moment, with what you have done in the past. And there is a connection with the future based on what you do in the present. This is karma. It has nothing to do with luck. No matter how slight your good or bad thoughts or actions are, they will still create negative or positive karma.

When the true you emerges (your awakening), you will be able to witness your karma continuing to play itself out, until it is dead and gone. Then, there is no new karma created after that.

The best thing you can do right now, is to create good karma as much as you can. You can do this through kindness to others, helping others, treating the environment well, keeping a positive attitude and continuing with Thought Watching and Breath Watching which will make you a happy and content person and, in turn, be an inspiration to everyone that you come in contact with. Change yourself and you change the world.

Bad karma is synonymous with stress. Living an honest, moral life limits the possibility for acquiring bad karma or remorse. Be clear about your motives and actions. Be truthful. These strengthen concentration leading to discernment of what is skilful or not, leading to the true you and the enlightened mind.

Be aware of your ever changing mental qualities.

10 KARMA CONNECTING YOUR PAST TO YOUR FUTURE

You could be restricted, scattered, concentrated, doubtful, fearful or dull and then a short time later, it is completely different. Your mastery of concentration comes a lot quicker when you go with the flow. If you are feeling really scattered, uncertain or aloof, then that isn't a good time to hone your skills. But when you are feeling focused, concentrated or positive, that would be a great time to seize the moment, and take note of how you are improving every minute.

Give yourself a little pat on the back once in a while. Just remember not to cling to that good feeling of accomplishment. The good feeling may stay with you for a while without you needing to coax it or trying to hold onto it. I said it before and I'll say it again, that happiness is already within you.

Observe yourself and stay true to yourself. There is plenty of advice from others. Other people who consider themselves, or they are considered by others, to be experts. There are scientific studies and evaluations. They are merely opinions. They are opinions based solely within their framework of their own knowledge and imagination. Don't allow others to dictate your own beliefs.

Accept things as they are, not as you want them to

be. These are words to live by. It does not mean that you can't go about working on changing something. It just means that you are accepting that it is what it is. So even when you are faced with negative feelings and emotions about something, you allow it. You accept it. You are at peace. And when you are at peace, you are much clearer minded to change what you want to change.

For most people, it is very difficult to grasp this concept. But the reward is great if you do. But if you don't, you go on struggling. You carry the burden. You remain stressed out.

Why is it so difficult to understand and implement a new way of thinking? Just look at how many years you have spent reinforcing the belief that all your negative feelings and emotions must be either prevented or gotten rid of when you get them. If you're sad, people tell you to, "Cheer up." If you're stressed out, people tell you to, "Do something to take your mind off of it," or to, "Relax."

You struggle to remain a positive thinker. You struggle to remain happy. You struggle to stop struggling. Remember all the times you said, "I give up?" You were trying to accept things, and ease your stress. Unfortunately, it made you feel like a failure, and that started the whole cycle over again, with negative feelings.

There is depressing news every day. There is violence. There is poverty. There are mean and nasty people. There is never enough money to do what you want. There is sickness. There is death of loved ones. There are thorns on the stem of a rose. But the rose smells wonderful and the rose is beautiful. You looked past, you were accepting, that the thorns were there. The rose lives in perfect harmony with its thorns and its beauty... and so should you.

Let go of your struggle to exist. Let go of your struggle to improve. Let go of your struggle to change. Let go of your struggle to achieve. Let go of your struggle to acquire. Let go of your struggle to understand. I've helped you to cross the flood and get to the other shore. Now you must get off of the raft and let that go too.

The truth (the true you), the answers (your key to happiness), the beginning and end of time (this is your life, in the present moment), are right here, right now (find and you shall no longer seek).

Made in the USA
Charleston, SC
01 October 2013